19/9.

The Church of England

EDWARD WILLIAM WATSON

Epilogue by
ALWYN WILLIAMS
LORD BISHOP OF WINCHESTER

Third Edition

LONDON
OXFORD UNIVERSITY PRESS
NEW YORK   TORONTO
1961

Oxford University Press, Amen House, London E.C.4

GLASGOW NEW YORK TORONTO MELBOURNE WELLINGTON
BOMBAY CALCUTTA MADRAS KARACHI KUALA LUMPUR
CAPE TOWN IBADAN NAIROBI ACCRA

First edition 1914
Second edition 1944
Third edition 1961

PRINTED IN GREAT BRITAIN

PREFATORY NOTE TO SECOND EDITION

THE author of this book, Dr. E. W. Watson, some-time Canon of Christ Church and Regius Professor of Ecclesiastical History in the University of Oxford, was born in 1859 and died in 1936. He was a scholar of wide and curious learning, who to the great loss of history committed little of it to paper. This was the more unfortunate because his judgement was keen and balanced, and his pen trenchant. His principal writings were a treatise on Cyprian's language and style and an admirable *Life* of Bishop John Wordsworth. It would be a service to knowledge to collect some of his articles and reviews written for such periodicals as the *English Historical Review*, the *Church Quarterly Review*, and the *Journal of Theological Studies*. They show the same cool pithy wisdom which few, though they may disagree in opinion, will fail to enjoy in this little book on the Church of England. Dr. Watson was especially interested in parishes and their history: this interest comes out clearly here. But he knew his whole subject as few have known it. The present writer was honoured by the request to write an Epilogue for this new impression, and he has done so. But he cannot draw Ulysses' bow.

ALWYN DUNELM

1943

NOTE TO THIRD EDITION

IN this third edition a few slight alterations have been made in Dr. Watson's text: none of them affects his opinion or judgement: they have simply been necessitated by the passing of the years, and involve little more than some changes of tense and one or two matters of dating and expression. The Epilogue has been revised and in parts rewritten, but retains its original character. The Bibliography has been modestly enlarged to include some recent books of special value.

ALWYN WINTON

1960

CONTENTS

		PAGE
PREFATORY NOTE		5
CHAPTER		
I. THE ANGLO-SAXON PERIOD		7
II. THE MEDIAEVAL SYSTEM		26
III. THE DECAY OF THE MEDIAEVAL SYSTEM		61
IV. THE BEGINNING OF THE REFORMATION		77
V. THE REIGN OF ELIZABETH		91
VI. THE STUARTS		102
VII. THE EIGHTEENTH CENTURY		121
VIII. THE NINETEENTH CENTURY		139
EPILOGUE 1914–60. BY ALWYN WILLIAMS, D.D., BISHOP OF WINCHESTER		171
BIBLIOGRAPHY		187
INDEX		189

CHAPTER I

THE ANGLO-SAXON PERIOD

THE history of the English Church begins with the conversion to Christianity of the English people. There were already Christians in all parts of Great Britain; where the English had conquered and settled there was a minority of serfs; elsewhere a Celtic population that was either independent or under English domination. But these Christians were to have, at the utmost, an influence upon English Christianity; they were not to control its structure or its character.

The conversion of the English was not an isolated event. It was part of a change through which all the Teutonic races that won new homes in what had been the Roman Empire had passed or were to pass. Latin Christianity for them represented a higher life, in morals and civilization, than that of their fathers. Its faith, preached as universally true and necessary for salvation, its worship, impressively carried out, struck their imagination and gained their assent. This Christianity was one. There was no thought that Christians could be Christian in different ways, or as members of different communions. Even when there were disputes and misunderstandings, as there were at first between English and Celtic Christians in England, they were at one in principle. The only dispute was as to the true following of the rule which all agreed must exist; they would never have consented to differ in belief or in the organization of their Church. This unity was the lesson that had been impressed upon Christians by great doctrinal struggles through which agreement in faith had been reached, and by the training in uniformity of administration which they had received from the Roman Empire, under which their system had grown up and after whose pattern it had been largely shaped. In theory and in practice there was one faith and one organization, though the former might not always be intelligently held nor the latter efficiently administered.

There was nothing strange in the resolution of Gregory the Great to send a mission for the conversion of England. As a Christian, as Bishop of Rome and head of the predominant Church in the western world, it was natural that he should do so, and he had good reason to expect success. Gregory was a man of ardent faith and great governing power. He was also the leading writer and thinker of his day, and had no small share in lowering European thought to the level of the Dark Ages. But this, for practical purposes, only made him the more effective. His general outlook, and that of his followers, was so near to the thought of his future English converts that no great incongruity could be felt when the Christian range of ideas came to be added to that which they had inherited.

In 596 Gregory sent forth his mission, which reached England in the following year. The leader, St. Augustine, had some forty followers. He was himself the abbot whom they were implicitly to obey: as soon as he should have won converts and have founded a Church, he was charged to obtain episcopal orders that he might rule it. The chief members of the mission were monks, like their chief; this fact, and the smallness of their number, were to be of decisive importance for the history of the Church. As monks they could be at home only in their monastery; they could not settle down here and there to pastoral charges. And the clergy under the control of the head of the mission were, and continued to be, quite inadequate in number to undertake such duties.

But this was a difficulty of the future. The success

of Augustine was immediate. He landed in Kent, the nearest and, as it happened, the most important of the English kingdoms. King Ethelbert had already a Christian wife, and was soon persuaded to become a Christian himself. The story of his conversion has often been told, and need not be repeated here. For us the important fact is that his people copied him. They were in the tribal stage; where the chief led the people followed. This is true of all the kingdoms in turn and not of Kent only. The old religion had been but lightly held; we hear as little of persistent adherence to paganism as we do of persecution for accession to the new faith. The policy of the mission was, in fact, that of the great Jesuit, St. Francis Xavier, a thousand years later in the East. The people were first to be secured by baptism, and then to be instructed. The result was that a multitude of superstitions passed into English Christianity and were but slowly purged out, their final decay dating rather from the Civil War of the seventeenth century than from the Reformation.

But if the Christian faith was lightly accepted, it was on occasion as lightly dropped. When Essex, one of the first districts to be converted, lost its Christian king and he was succeeded by sons who reverted to paganism, their people followed the example and the East Saxons were among the last of the English to become permanently Christian. Such a reaction was exceptional and temporary, but the work of conversion was superficial. It needed, if it were to be effectual, a systematic supervision and instruction of the converts, and there were none to give it. Within the convents which were quickly established there was a sheltered life of singular purity and devotion. The Venerable Bede, to whom we owe the *Ecclesiastical History of the People of the English*, a masterpiece of primitive history such as no other nation in Europe can boast, and who was also through many laborious compilations the instructor in all its sciences of the early Middle Ages, shows this early Church at its best. But outside the convent there was little provision of Christian teaching. From the cathedral monasteries the bishops and their clergy made tours, more or less comprehensive, through the dioceses, and in course of time there arose, under episcopal government, a certain number of central churches which came to be called the 'Old Minsters'. To them the Christians brought their children to be baptized, there the worship was worthily and regularly performed, and priests might always be found. But such churches were few and far between, and their clergy could not know and visit the people of the isolated and self-centred villages that sprang up in the English backwoods.

There was obvious need for a local clergy, and not only was there a need, from a Christian point of view, but the converts had been accustomed while still pagan to a local priesthood, and expected their new religion to provide it under the changed conditions. Among all the Teutonic tribes it was the custom that the chief or lord should have a temple of his own for his pagan worship, and that it should be occupied by a priest of his appointment. At that temple his dependants had to worship, and to it they brought their customary offerings. It was a source of profit to the lord, who was its owner and the master of the priest. But the latter had normally a further income on which he could depend. He had a double share in the fields of the village community, holding two 'yardlands' while the ordinary villager held only one. He was a husbandman, ploughing and reaping like the rest, though not burdened with the task of labouring, as they did, on the lord's land. He was bound by a strange usage that prevailed in all Teutonic countries, to supply a bull and a boar for the service of the village. With pagan belief the pagan priest disappeared. But the acres were there, demanding a priest to till them, and the community felt itself incomplete unless it had its worship. However, this provision could only be enjoyed on the lord's terms. He had nominated, and he continued to nominate, the priest. The church, according to the theory of English law, was his freehold down to the fifteenth century, and for some time after the Norman Conquest he continued to regard it as a source of profit. The chapter of St. Paul's Cathedral, who had been endowed with many London churches by benefactors, used in the twelfth century to lease them out, either to a priest or to a lay person who employed a priest to conduct the services, at a rental which might on the average amount, in modern values, to £100 a year. As for the bull and the boar, they were still provided in the eighteenth century by the rectors of hundreds of English parishes.

Thus the Christian priest stepped into the place of his pagan predecessor. The lord named him, the bishop ordained him. But for generations the bishop did nothing more. He was not one of the bishop's staff; he was not, and could not be in his lonely position in a roadless land, kept under supervision. There were no rural deans and few archdeacons before the Norman Conquest, and bishops kept no registers of their proceedings till the thirteenth century. They had little means of knowing who were the parish clergy, and there is small reason to suppose that they regarded it as their duty to know.

But, such as it was, this provision of local clergy satisfied the people and was steadily augmented. Till after the Norman Conquest the number grew as village after village was formed; there are counties, such as Norfolk and Dorset, where parishes, each with its priest, were more numerous in the twelfth century than they are to-day. For each little community felt that it was incomplete without its priest; he was as necessary to its corporate life as the miller or the smith. In fact, the density of our early population may be measured by the number of parishes. As we travel north and west we find them increasing in acreage. Moor and fen and forest will account in part for the sparsity; but we may probably assume that great parishes like Leeds and Sheffield, in what were Celtic regions to a comparatively late period, represent the religious provision needed by a small number of English invaders. Their position would be similar to that of the scattered Protestants in the west of Ireland, and the older population would satisfy its requirements in forgotten ways, which may be represented by some of the ancient chapelries within such parishes.

Clergy were provided; a congregation also was provided. The church was the lord's; it was property, and a source of income. As it was his, the duty of attending it, and so augmenting its receipts, was incumbent upon his men and their families. But how were the duties of the priest fulfilled? We must bear in mind that primarily his task was not to teach or to influence, but to do for his people what they could not do for themselves. He administered the sacraments, and often he stumbled with difficulty through the Latin words. There is even evidence of priests who repeated the sounds without knowing their meaning. There is evidence also that many priests in their daily life were on the level of the little farmers by whose side they worked on the land; that there was grossness and drunkenness. But among priests and people there was a deep and undoubting conviction, darkened by much fear, of the truths of their religion;

and it was not the less sincere that it was mingled with incongruous elements of the older religion and that primitive passions were stubborn. At its best, as seen in some of the numerous homilies—written to be delivered by the unlearned clergy—that have survived, the faith of our ancestors was simple and evangelical, and bore good fruit in life.

The basis of the system was the village community and its priest. He was dependent, as we have seen, upon the lord and independent of the bishop. One of the most important lines of development in the history of our Church has been that by which the priest has gained independence and stability as against the lord, who has dwindled into the 'patron', while he has in great measure retained his independence of the bishop. The 'parson's freehold' goes far back towards the beginning of English Christianity. But the authority of the bishop, if it extends to-day, with limitations, over all the working clergy, is confined in other respects within narrower bounds than in the early times.

We must bear in mind that the first missionaries came as bearers not only of the Gospel but of a new civilization. Their counsel was desired in all matters of importance. The English of the sixth century were about at the same stage of development as the most intelligent African tribes of 1914, and they were eager to advance, and to advance by imitation. Under Christian influence they first framed codes of law, or rather of custom. Life and death and the sanctity of marriage were among the issues at stake, and the heads of the Church must needs desire to make their influence felt. They were ready to give their counsel, and ready (as missionaries in many lands and of many communions have been in modern times) to accept such a position as should give them place and weight in public affairs. That place could only be held by the bishop; his monks were under vows of obedience to him, while he was free. So the bishops received great grants of land, and the second place, each in the kingdom to which his see belonged, next after the king. There was a religious side to all administrative work, and so they assisted in the general affairs of government and claimed that in return government should concern itself with the affairs of the Church. The national assembly was the place of decision for business of both kinds, and kings and their wise men were apt to be conspicuous even in ecclesiastical councils. The age, in fact, was too primitive to draw the fine distinction between Church and State. In the earliest days the results were good; justice and mercy were more likely to prevail when the bishops made their voices heard than when lay passions were uncontrolled. But later, when kingdoms grew few and finally but one remained, the relative importance of the bishop declined, and he tended to become almost a minister of state; once at least in the Anglo-Saxon Chronicle bishops are bluntly classed among the 'king's thegns'. Even the reformers among them, who did much to revive the monastic life, and to make the English cloisters a pattern of piety and learning for the west of Europe, were powerless to govern the parish clergy. In fact, they made no such attempt. On their great estates they did not keep control of church life, but allowed the same system of an independent parochial ministry to grow up as on the estates of laymen. They had no other security for its efficiency than their own right of appointment. Even the original centres from which their staff had worked, the 'Old Minsters', were abandoned, and became ordinary parochial churches in the bishop's patronage.

The parish and the diocese were weak points in the system, but we must bear in mind that efficiency of administration is the modern rediscovery of an art which was lost with the fall of the Roman Empire, and that throughout the Middle Ages government, except for strenuous intervals, was weak. Nor was the higher control of the Church effective. Gregory the Great, when he sent his monks to convert England, was quite in the dark as to the local conditions. He knew from books that when the greater part of Britain was under Roman rule London and York were its chief cities. His plan was that each of the two was to be the seat of an archbishop with twelve suffragans. These two provinces were to be co-ordinate and independent, the senior archbishop for the time being taking precedence, and they with their bishops were to take counsel together from time to time. In 597 all Celtic Britain was Christian, and it does not appear on what terms Gregory expected it and its bishops to fall in with his scheme. Those who were nearest to Canterbury, the Welsh, would not; and York was long unable to extend its influence northward, and never succeeded in effectively controlling the bishops of what was afterwards the one kingdom of Scotland. As yet there was no sign that the island was to be divided between two, and only two, kingdoms, or that the divisions would be in a true sense national. But of slighter, though effective, divisions there were so many, both in the north and in the south, that the first six Archbishops of Canterbury failed to establish any provincial system at all. Missionaries came from various quarters, Birinus to Wessex from North Italy, Felix from Burgundy to East Anglia; most notable of all, St. Aidan and his colleagues from Iona to the north of England, whence their influence and that of their English disciples, such as St. Chad, spread over the Midlands. There was no unity; even the workers from the Continent came independently, without asking the consent or receiving the aid of the successors

of St. Augustine. The evangelists from the north
were out of communion with the rest, ostensibly on
points of practice, such as the date of Easter, really on
the point of authority. They, like the Welsh, refused
to allow that the newcomers had any right, on the
ground of their commission from Rome, to exercise
authority over the British Churches.

There was, then, in practice no officer superior to
the tribal bishop; and in the Celtic missions the bishop
himself was, at least in theory, subordinate to the
Abbot of Iona. This want of system was remedied
by the great Archbishop Theodore of Tarsus (667–
690). He came with the glamour of a direct commission from Rome, and his native land was one where
full episcopal rule of the normal type prevailed as in
the great days of St. Athanasius and St. Chrysostom.
He determined that he would not hold an empty
office; he would be a real metropolitan. He started
with a great advantage. The Northern English had
just decided at the Council of Whitby, in 663, that they
would give up their Celtic peculiarities of observance.
By so deciding they practically put themselves under
Canterbury, for York, as an archbishopric, had had a
brief life of five years (628–633) ending in disaster,
and when Northumbrian Christianity had revived it
it had been after the Celtic pattern, which recked little
of ecclesiastical order. York for the next seventy
years was merely a bishopric, and as such attracted
Theodore's attention. In his home, as everywhere
where the canonical discipline had grown up after the
pattern of Roman Imperial government, the bishop
towards his clergy was in the position of the prefect
in a French department towards his officials. He was
their master, and they had few rights as against him.
Theodore evidently wished to make episcopal control
real in England, and to this end he set to work to

reduce the size of the bishoprics. Among those which he divided was York. Wilfrid of York had been the leader on the side of Roman observance at Whitby. He felt that he was wronged, and he was not the man to submit. He appealed, confident of success, to Rome. The Pope, he was sure, would not allow the champion of Roman worship to be robbed of two-thirds of his diocese. Wilfrid had no scruples over its extent, and, in fact, dioceses wide in area were as primitive in certain regions as small ones in others. There was a famous Syrian bishop of the fifth century who had eight hundred parishes in his. Wilfrid may also have realized, what was the truth, that it was Utopian to dream of episcopal control over parish priests who were subordinate to their lords and independent of the bishop. In any case, Rome supported Wilfrid against Canterbury, but quite in vain. The English kings were on Theodore's side, and Wilfrid, after long struggles and exiles, in one of which he converted the last pagans in England, those of Sussex and the Isle of Wight, had finally to submit to a humiliating compromise. Theodore had his way. He also succeeded for a moment in establishing a true union of the English Church, in the form of councils to be held annually. But this was in advance of his time and quickly broke down; while he failed in his advocacy of a scheme, for which England even now is not ripe, that the number of bishoprics should increase regularly with the number of Christians. Neither kings nor bishops nor the English at large wished for the bureaucratic episcopacy of the Roman Empire. This purpose of a united Church was finally thwarted when in 735 the Northumbrians raised the bishopric of York to an archbishopric, with a province of its own. Since then, save on rare and irregular occasions, as when Cardinal Wolsey, as Papal legate,

B

presided over a council of both provinces, there was
no attempt to bring all England together for Church
purposes till the creation in 1904 of the 'Representative
Church Council', which had no legislative powers.
The mischief of duality has been mitigated by the
comparative unimportance of the York Convocation,
which has seldom taken a line of its own in opposition
to Canterbury.

Canterbury was the child of Rome. St. Augustine
had been sent from Rome to found the English Church,
and though he was allowed a free hand, neither
Gregory nor he forgot the relation between them.
Nor could English Christians forget the reverence
universally paid to Rome. As yet the two Apostles,
St. Peter and St. Paul, shared the honour that was paid
to their place of martyrdom, but ecclesiastical policy
was already beginning to be fortified by theological
considerations which augmented the regard for St.
Peter at the cost of his brother Apostle. Rome was
not only the greatest Church in Christendom, but also
the model Church; as yet those lapses which were to
tarnish its renown were in the future. The bishops of
Rome made the most of a position and an authority
which they were conscious of using for the general
benefit. Their relation to smaller Churches was
primarily like that of some great physician from St.
Bartholomew's who may visit a county hospital.
The words of such a dignitary must be received with
respect, whether they be of praise or reproof. Then
there grew up a system of ecclesiastical order, with the
bishop of Rome at the head of the hierarchy, and as
both he and the other bishops were concerned with
religious matters, this hierarchical arrangement came
to be itself regarded as having a religious sanction.
Then came theological explanation of the observed
facts. Just as the astronomers of those ages were quite

right in their observations of the stars, but erred in the hypotheses they framed to account for the facts, so it was with the theologians. They worked out their hypothesis to account for the Pope's position in Christendom, and have ended by putting it into their creed. The earlier among them laboured under the difficulty of grasping so abstract an idea as a Church or a corporation with continuous succession. They could only put their case in a personal form. When the Roman Church appealed to some secular potentate for help it made St. Peter write in his own name. It was not a mere rhetorical artifice; their mental outlook was the same as that of the Domesday clerks who recorded that St. Paul (meaning the chapter of St. Paul's) was unjustly occupying some lands in Essex. This naïve personification was very impressive, and did much to enhance the reverence for the Roman see. Though the theological process was still incomplete in Anglo-Saxon times, the reverence, though vague, was intense, and not the less because contact was but intermittent. Roman bishops took little thought for a Church concerning which they had small opportunity of making their will effectual, or even of making it known, and wisely abstained from counsels that were likely to be ignored. And there were intervals when Rome was in a discreditable state, and when it was well that few pilgrims should learn and repeat the truth about papal escapades. So Rome was respected in an indefinite way, and subsidized by handsome gifts from time to time and by an annual payment, from the eighth century onwards, of 'Peter's Pence', which Rome came to regard as a tribute and an evidence of England's dependence.

The great Archbishop Theodore not only introduced, so far as he could, ecclesiastical order; he also introduced Roman civilization. Wilfrid also was active in the same cause. The schools of Canterbury and York, the latter itself a child of Bede's school at Jarrow, first acquired the full wisdom of the age and then handed it on to the Continent as well as to Britain. English scholarship did service to the future by the art of copying, and so preserving, ancient documents, an art that has never reached higher levels than in some English MSS., notably the Codex Amiatinus of the Bible now preserved at Florence, the noblest though not the most ornate of Latin manuscripts. English scholars also popularized the knowledge of the age, scientific, literary, historical, as well as theological, and diffused it through Western Europe. The greatest of all was Alcuin, the master of schools for Charles the Great. Englishmen also in the same period, the century or thereabouts that followed the death of Theodore in 690, did imperishable service in the conversion of Western Germany by Boniface and Willehad, the first from Devonshire, the second from Northumbria. Boniface was the greater, for his converts were voluntary and he suffered martyrdom (755); Willehad preached to Saxons who were forced to listen and to accept baptism by their conqueror, Charles the Great. The great sees of Mainz and Bremen owe their origin to these Englishmen, and many of their countrymen shared their labours.

This second exertion of Roman influence carried the work of St. Augustine to a higher level than the English Church could maintain. There was from the middle of the eighth century a steady decline, chiefly due, no doubt, to the absence of any supervision that might keep the English up to the mark. They were mentally in the schoolboy stage, and there was no master for them. Rome itself, even Rome at its best, was sinking into the same mental state, and neither Rome nor any other agency was systematically con-

trolling them. The Church became more secular and
the monasteries more self-centred. Nor had the
influence of the great mission from Iona been lasting.
It would be unjust not to value very highly the saintliness and zeal of its leaders; but its working had been
intensive rather than diffusive, at least on English soil,
and within the lifetime of Bede, who died in 735, there
was a deep decline. While the Church was thus in a
falling state, as Christians of Africa might have been in
this century if European aid were withdrawn, there fell
upon England the last great outburst of pagan savagery.
The Scandinavian Vikings first attacked England in
793. The old civilization, such as it was, perished.
The monasteries were destroyed or deserted, the
clergy became illiterate, bishops became leaders in
battle and allowed themselves the liberties of the
soldier. The noble efforts of King Alfred to restore
learning and create a vernacular literature had a certain
success, but from this time forth the utmost that was
done was to recover some of the lost ground. We
cannot regard the later Anglo-Saxon period as one of
progress in Church or State.

The revival, so far as we know, was confined to the
monasteries and the monastic cathedrals. Of the
latter many during the generations of disorder had
abandoned any pretence of monastic order. Their
clergy lived as canons (the word first appears in
England in 787): i.e. clergy, not under vows, who
lived together voluntarily under a certain degree of
discipline. This discipline was very loose, and it
became common for the canons to occupy houses of
their own and to take wives, though the foundations
that supported them had been endowed for the maintenance of monks. In the tenth century there came
a revival of the Benedictine ideal; English enthusiasts
entered French or Flemish monasteries to learn the

practice of the rule, and returned to establish it in
English houses. Bishops and kings were among the
supporters of the movement; among them was not
St. Dunstan, who, rigorous monk as he was, did not
disturb the canons who in his day were in possession
of his cathedral at Canterbury. It was not till after
his day that Canterbury became once more monastic;
and some of the greatest cathedrals, such as York and
St. Paul's, were never restored to monasticism. Of
the monasteries that were not cathedral, few, if any,
have a continuous monastic life stretching beyond the
Danish invasions. Even the greatest, such as Glastonbury, had passed through a phase in which they had
been mere colonies of secular clergy, living more or
less canonically. But the revival, when it came—and
it came too late to save many of the ancient foundations from falling into lay hands and so perishing—
was a real one, the final glory of Anglo-Saxon Christianity. Of monastic life for women we know little.
Houses for them were comparatively few; their
inmates were honoured, and they were often governed
by ladies of royal blood.

The century before the Norman Conquest was one
of increasing secularity. Disaster under Ethelred
the Unready and foreign domination under Cnut and
his sons demoralized the England over which Edward
the Confessor ruled weakly. If the Church had the
honour of a martyr in St. Alphage, slain by the heathen
Danes in 1012, it was sadly in need of reform, and not
least at the head. There came to be more and more
of secularity among the bishops. For the bishops were
in practice selected by the sovereign, whether with
or without the assent of his wise men, and with or
without the form of an election by the clergy. These
restrictions upon the king's liberty of choice, which
even in the earlier times may not have had much

reality, tended in the later to disappear. For the bishop held so important, and, it must be added, so wealthy, an office that the king could not well allow freedom of choice. And if the bishop was a counsellor, and often a minister, of state, still more was the archbishop. Canterbury and York were thrones whose occupants could not be chosen on purely religious grounds; it is but justice to say that there is no reason to think that they were given for purely non-religious reasons.

We find then, at the end of the Anglo-Saxon period, a Church in grave need of reform. Its heads, the bishops, were national or at least local leaders quite as much as they were ecclesiastics; in its monasteries, probably its most satisfactory element, were living monks and nuns whose lives were serious and their employments worthy of their calling, though there was not the enthusiasm among them nor the new efficiency and scholarship that had recently been kindled on the Continent. Its parish clergy had certainly ceased to be as dependent on their lord as they had been in the early days of the Conversion, but there is no reason to think that any preliminary training was thought needful before they were ordained, or that they were expected, by the bishop or any one else, to differ in mode of life from their brother-farmers. It is needless to say that they were usually married; so were many canons and some bishops. But in one respect their status had certainly risen; they had come to be in many cases recipients of tithe, and thus their social position, especially in regard to their lord, had been improved. And recent study has tended in many other ways to modify harsh judgements upon the last century of the Anglo-Saxon Church.

Tithe is widely, and quite wrongly, regarded as a source of income that was devised for the benefit of the local clergy, and has often been unjustly withdrawn from them. Historically, this is untrue. Tithe-paying to the clergy was first inculcated in the fourth century, after the idea became prevalent that the three orders of the Christian ministry correspond to the three of the Jewish, and hence, like the Jewish of old, have a right to tithe. It was a moral duty to pay tithe of all gain, even of plunder taken in war; Abraham had set an example here. But the poor also had an obvious claim upon funds that were given as a matter of religious duty; and in the Roman Empire, where each diocese was centralized under a bishop, he was the natural trustee for sums contri-buted to either purpose. In the empire of the Franks, which succeeded the Roman, religious pressure became more and more emphatic, but still the obligation long remained a moral one. But tithe came to mean more precisely tithe upon land when Frankish kings in the sixth and seventh centuries formed the habit of granting a tenth of the produce of parts of their dominions to bishops and religious houses. One of the chief sources of State revenue under the Roman Empire and its Frankish successor had been this tax of a tenth, and now in places it fell to the Church, or rather to particular churches. Then, in 765, a general law was made by Pepin the Short, a Frankish king, that this whole tax should in future be an ecclesiastical revenue. This was in recompense for a wholesale seizure of Church lands which his father had per-petrated. From this time onward tithe of the produce of land dwarfed all other tithe in importance, and practically tithe came to mean the tithe on land.

The little English kingdoms looked to the great Frankish dominion as their model, and tithe soon became law in England. At a national council, held under the presidency of a Papal legate in 787, it was ordered that all were to pay tithe, and this was made compulsory by the sanction given by the three chief English kings, those of Mercia, Wessex, and Northumbria. This was a general obligation, without specific reference to land, and Anglo-Saxon administration was so weak that it certainly could not be systematically enforced. The law was made definite under Athelstan, who ordered that tithe should be paid from land, and appointed the recipients. Two-thirds were to go to the 'Old Minster', i.e. to the bishop's general fund. He was master of the 'Old Minsters', and their clergy were under him. One-third was to go to the private church, if there were one. If there were not, the whole was to go to the 'Old Minster'. This scheme soon broke down. The bishops abandoned the personal supervision of their dioceses exercised through the clergy of the 'Old Minsters', which simply became parish churches, and so had small claim to tithe from lords and people for whom they did nothing. Thus the landowners ceased to support these 'Old Minsters' with their tithe, except those who, with their people, still attended at them. The others in many cases paid their whole tithe to their local priest; not only did this seem a just return for his services, but it was in the interest of the lord. It increased the value of the office to which he appointed. Nor did the bishops resent it. They had ample revenues of their own to maintain themselves and their central cathedral staff, and they were no longer interested in the 'Old Minsters'. But the lords were not obliged to confer this favour on their own priests, and many, especially among the smaller, may have had no priest. Thus their tithe was at their own disposal. They must pay it, but they might pay it to whom they would. About the time of the Norman Conquest much tithe was free in this way. But by the thirteenth century the idea had become prevalent that a tithe-payer who was not pledged to some other recipient was bound to give his tithe to the parish priest, and this under Innocent III, who died in 1216, became the general law of Western Christendom, in England as elsewhere.

CHAPTER II

THE MEDIAEVAL SYSTEM

THE Norman Conquest of 1066 brought England into close contact with Europe. Our ancestors had suffered from isolation; they had a literature in their own tongue such as no other nation could boast, but on the religious side they had little else. Not that they were below the general level in regard to faith or life, but that they had been in a back-water, unaffected by modern currents of progress. They were powerless to bring their two institutions of the private church and the episcopate into a working relation. A solution of that problem was already being attempted on the Continent, and the Norman Conquest meant that in England the same attempt should be made. It is true that in general civilization and in its religious state Normandy was in no better order than England. The Normans had only just begun to be civilized, and their bishops and clergy were rude and military. But their monasteries were in advance of the age. No higher examples of disciplined devoutness could be found than in them, and it was good that the impulse should be transmitted to England. Normans had furnished the earnestness, but not the gift to turn it to good account. It was their contact with the wider world that had brought Italians, Lanfranc and Anselm, to settle among them. They did not come as aliens, for as yet the Roman imperial tradition of universal citizenship had not been ousted by the idea of nationality. It was the counterpart of the universal churchmanship of the age; and, indeed, a great deal that is often called catholic might better be styled cosmopolitan. The Normans welcomed such messengers of a higher life, and accepted their teaching. That teaching, so far as we are concerned, was the mediaeval doctrine of Church and State.

European society was feudal in its organization. Everybody was somebody's man, till the apex was reached where sat the monarch, responsible only to God. We have seen how in the Teutonic countries, such as England, the parish priest was the man of his lord. That relation had grown weaker as time advanced and as Church property had come to be regarded as more and more sacred. It was now believed to belong to the altar, and the lord, though he had wide powers of choice as to the recipient to whom he would grant it, dared not use it, or allow it to be used, for other than ecclesiastical purposes. But the thought of lordship had not stopped short at the parochial clergy. Kings, or (on the Continent) great nobles, regarded bishops as their men, and held that they granted them the office as well as its emoluments. The essential thing was the grant; the consecration was its sequel, necessary, no doubt, but merely a consequence. At the head of the ideal system was the Emperor, who was in practice master of Germany and in theory—often it was no more than theory—lord of Italy and Rome. In the first half of the eleventh century the Emperors had nominated several Popes in succession. Those Popes had been well chosen, and had worked a much-needed reform in the Papacy, the consequence of which was an increase in the estimate which the world and the Popes themselves had of their office. But England, unlike the Pope, needed to pay no attention to the Emperor's theoretical claims.

A strong and self-respecting Papacy was a benefit to the age. For the feudal idea had lowered the standard of clerical, and especially of episcopal, life and work. In France and in Germany, more than in England, bishops were men of the rough world in which they lived. How were they to be recalled to the standard of their profession? Only by the establishment of a rival feudal system, clerical from top to bottom, with a loyalty of its own and a sense of duty from inferior to superior, the apex of the system being the representative of God on earth, responsible only to Him. So would the clergy be detached from their degrading contact with the world. But this system required that not only the persons but the properties of the clergy should be severed from worldly connexion, and here the difficulty began. For that property was secure only by the protection of the State, and in return for that protection the State had a claim upon its holders. It needed financial support, and it needed also the counsel of the leaders of the Church. And the State put that demand into a feudal form. The heads of the Church were 'tenants-in-chief', holding lands directly from the Crown, and putting them to profit by granting them out to knights and others who owed to their clerical superiors exactly the same duties as if those superiors had been earls or barons. And it must be said that many bishops, and good men among them, were quite as much interested in these secular duties and their emoluments as in their ecclesiastical position, and quite as loyal to the King as to the Pope, to the head of the worldly as of the churchly hierarchy. If a conflict of duties arose, it would inevitably be a sharp one.

The feudal scheme of the Church was in some important respects successfully carried through. This was notably the case with the parish clergy. They became the bishop's men, in the feudal sense, and so they have continued. The promise of canonical obedience and the act of institution are thoroughly feudal. So feudal was the relation between bishop and beneficed clergy that it gave the bishop the same right of levying an 'aid' from them that a lay lord had in regard to those who held under him. When he had to meet special expenses, such as the payment of fees to Rome, or the discharge of heavy debts, the bishop acted like the knight who was called out to war or had to provide a marriage portion for his eldest daughter. He passed on as much of the cost as he could to his subordinates. This feudal right even survived the Reformation; a bishop of Lichfield exercised it in 1582. Thus in a real sense the parish clergy had changed their position; they became the men not of the lord who had appointed them, but of the bishop. This change—a change in opinion as well as in practice—was effected soon after the Norman Conquest. We must not, however, over-estimate its importance. For a lord, according to feudal principles, had no arbitrary rights over his men. So long as they did their duty he had to protect them; he could not displace them nor meddle with their property. Thus the change actually strengthened the position of the clergy. It became even more a 'freehold' than before. The lord's position, again, did not deteriorate. His right to nominate the parson was unaffected; he had to nominate him, it is true, to the bishop, who performed the act of admission to the benefice, but the bishop had and still has only limited powers of objecting to the patron's nominee. The further, and originally unlimited, powers of the lord had lost all practical value before they were superseded by the new relation to the bishop.

But this new status both of bishop and patron had to be justified, and it was justified by a legal fiction which historically was baseless. It was asserted that parishes had arisen from the delegation by the bishop of his pastoral duty in parts of his diocese. That was true enough of the towns around the coasts of the Mediterranean, where the churches had originally had the bishop for their one pastor, and the parishes had been separated off one by one. It had never been true of Western Europe, nor of the primitive churches in Syria and Cappadocia from which Christianity had advanced to the west by way of Milan. But feudal thought, which assumed that the relation between lord and man began in a grant by the former, was compelled to postulate such a grant from bishop to priest. Equally unhistorical was the explanation given at this stage of the origin of ecclesiastical patronage. It was asserted that, in return for the generosity of a benefactor, he and his representatives were allowed by the Church to present a clerk to the bishop. As we have seen, glebe was a customary endowment, far too uniform in extent and too prevalent to owe its origin to individual acts of beneficence, while tithe was a universal obligation, though the payer had a wide choice as to the recipient.

Had the two feudal systems been exactly parallel there would have been a regular gradation upwards from the bishop through the archbishop to the Pope. But the Popes, like such kings as William I, were too masterful for this. As every Englishman, whoever his lord might be, was the man of the King, and could not shelter himself in case of disobedience by pleading

the orders of his immediate lord, so the Popes insisted
that every bishop was immediately under themselves.
They ignored the provincial system, so far as it might
conflict with their own universal competence. They
believed themselves to be, and mankind in the best
days of the mediaeval system unhesitatingly believed
them to be, the representatives of God on earth. That
belief, as time went on, was to be shattered by facts.

Before speaking of the conflict between this feudal
system of the Church and the rival feudalism of the
kingdom, it will be well to speak of the practical working of the former in regard to the endowments of the
Church. They came to be taxed in support of its
central government. The Crusades were not only
stimulated but organized by the Popes. They were
costly campaigns, which needed a central treasury, and
no one but the Pope was sufficiently impartial and
earnest to administer it with success. So the nations
of Europe accepted the burden, and grew familiar with
Roman taxation, both of clergy and laity. Soon Rome
needed funds for other military purposes. It aimed
at maintaining and enlarging its own Italian domains,
and at weakening the Emperors who, from their seat
of power in Germany, were striving to make themselves masters of Italy and the Pope. It came to be a
struggle for existence, for time after time the Emperors
in the eleventh and following centuries set up rival
Popes, who, though never permanently successful,
often for a while made themselves masters of Rome and
received the allegiance of a great part of central Europe.
Hence the legitimate Popes were constantly engaged in
stirring up civil war in Germany, in order to weaken
the attack on Italy, and their activity in this respect
ended in breaking up German unity. Now this great
Continental struggle was necessarily waged by the
Popes as a religious warfare. One of their weapons

was excommunication, and all who engaged in, or helped to pay for, the conflict were told that they were engaged in a Crusade against the enemies of God; though in fact it was the distraction of this warfare that ensured the failure of the real Crusades in the Holy Land.

The Popes required that the English should share the expense of this European Crusade. They had no great success with the laity; international politics were against them, for English kings in chronic hostility with France could not wish to throw Germany into the arms of France by actively helping the Pope. Hence the burden was chiefly thrown upon the clergy, who had to bear also their full share of national taxation. But in theory, as we have seen, the clergy belonged to another feudal system than that of the laity. Ought they, then, to be taxed by or with the laity, or ought they to tax themselves? And ought they at all to subsidise the feudal organism to which they did not belong? Both questions received a final answer in the reign of Edward I. The clergy were to tax themselves in their own assembly, their Convocation, which served the double purpose of voting taxes and transacting ecclesiastical business. But we must deal with Convocation hereafter. This self-taxation had important results. It led to the isolation of the clergy from Parliament, except in the case of the bishops and great abbots who sat in the Upper House as barons. The others, having no concern with public finance, one of the most important functions of Parliament, were able to gratify their self-consciousness as a separate and cosmopolitan order by staying away. There was another serious consequence. Kings and Popes alike taxed not the clergy as such but only the endowed clergy. Now the clergy, according to our modern ideas, were excessively numerous, and the beneficed among them were a minority. But since only those who had tithe and glebe were taxed, only they voted the taxes; and as only they were represented in Convocation, purely ecclesiastical business fell into their hands to the exclusion of the rest of the clergy. Till the Restoration of Charles II the clergy continued to tax themselves; then the right was abandoned by an informal agreement between Archbishop Sheldon of Canterbury and Lord Clarendon, and the clergy have since then been taxed with the laity. They justly received the vote for Parliament, but by a meaningless survival are still excluded from sitting in it. By another meaningless survival the unbeneficed clergy could not till 1921 vote for members of their Convocation, though they can, if elected, sit therein. So lasting in its effects has been this mediaeval arrangement, which also has preserved the separate existence of the two English provinces. Had there not been need for a machinery of clerical taxation, that of York could scarcely have survived.

The endowments of the Church, then, paid their share of national taxation and also contributed to Papal needs. When the claim was made by a Pope of more courage than discretion that Church property should be free from payment to the State, it was summarily rejected by Edward I. Archbishop Winchelsey was a Papalist. The clergy, he said, have two lords, but they owe more obedience to the spiritual than the temporal. The spiritual had bidden them pay taxes only to him. It was sound feudal doctrine; the supreme lord, responsible only to God, had spoken and must be obeyed. Those who paid to the King were excommunicated by the archbishop, as the Pope's representative. The King outlawed him and his supporters, seized their lands and soon got his way.

C

We must bear in mind that while the mediaeval system was at its best, from the Norman Conquest to the days of Edward I, the most respected part of the clergy was the monastic. It would be inaccurate to assert, as is sometimes done, that the monasteries were corporate bodies outside the practical system of the church. They were not so regarded. The most important monasteries were the cathedral bodies which had been recovered for the Benedictine life in the century before the Conquest. Their number was about equal to that of the cathedrals in which canons, who had in the dark days of Danish invasion taken the place of monks, maintained their position. If York and London and Lincoln had canons, Canterbury and Durham and Winchester had monks. The position of the bishop was the same in both. They were corporate bodies of which he was the head, and originally their members had much of the power which a cathedral chapter or the governing body of a College at Oxford or Cambridge to-day has in relation to its dean or head. In a monastic cathedral the position was paradoxical. Individually the monks were under obedience, with no right to a will of their own; collectively they were a counterpoise to the bishop. Where there were canons, not under vows, the case was simpler, but the chapter's influence was not less than that of cathedral monks. There was a cathedral in North Germany where the official acts of the bishop were not valid till the chapter's seal was attached to them. Though the bishop's powers were not so limited in England, this influence of the cathedral body was irksome to the first Norman prelates in England, and they brought it to an end by dissolving the partnership. St. Osmund of Salisbury and Thomas I of York, among others, divided the estates which hitherto had supported bishop and cathedral into two parts. The bishop uncontrolled disposed of the one, the chapter of the other. If they were monks, they now elected a cathedral prior, who was their actual head; if they were canons, they elected a dean to preside over them. And the property was often divided in a way that seems strange to us. The government of churches was regarded as part of it, and so it came about that many cathedrals, notably St. Paul's and Salisbury, exercised an episcopal authority over a number of parishes which was only abolished in 1836. In such parishes the dean, not the bishop, instituted the incumbents and, if they offended, sat in judgement upon them. It was only for such occasional functions as a confirmation that a bishop was needed, and neither duty nor courtesy required that the bishop of the diocese should be called in. With the separation of properties began that independent existence of cathedral chapters with which we are familiar, though the election of their dean has passed from them. When Henry VIII abolished cathedral monasteries, like the rest, he reconstituted them, together with the new cathedral bodies which he created, as cathedrals of the 'New Foundation' on the same lines as those of the 'Old Foundation', though with certain modifications.

But this mutual separation was only the beginning of the cathedral system, in England as in other countries. The Norman victors in England gave their winnings with lavish generosity to all the great churches. They were as liberal in endowing existing cathedrals as in founding new monasteries. Salisbury, for instance, obtained property, chiefly in the form of churches, scattered over England from Grantham in Lincolnshire to Ilfracombe in Devon. It had some fifty clergy who were members of the corporate body, and representatives of the original staff of the missionary bishop. There was no diocesan work for them now, and their financial interest had largely ceased to be local. The great church existed for its own services and its own staff. But these had to live, and it was too hard a task for a rudimentary book-keeping to collect and divide the total income derived from many sources. It was simpler to assign a single source to each member, and to distribute the remainder for the supply of particular needs. This was also the procedure of the monasteries; in the greater ones separate estates were assigned to the kitchen, the cellar, the supply of clothing, the lighting of the church, and so forth. So in the secular cathedrals each member of the corporation received his particular source of income, his prebend, of which he was prebendary—prebendary of Ilfracombe, for instance. If it were a church, he took the tithe. Why should he not? He was in orders, and tithe was regarded as a provision for priests and levites. The conscience of the payer was acquitted if a person in orders received it, even though that person did nothing for those whose labours raised the crops from which the tithe was taken. But in fact he did something, for he provided, by deputy if not personally, the service in the parish church. Normally it was by deputy, for the claim upon the prebendary of his cathedral was a stronger one than that of the parish. Soon the plan was adopted by which the 'vicar', or deputy, took the whole charge of the parish in return for a certain proportion, usually about a third, of the income, and received security of tenure by institution. Thus the prebendary became merely the patron, and was free to confine his attention to the cathedral. There his most obvious duty was to take part in singing the services, and the corporate body was large enough to provide choir as well as clergy. But the prebendaries were men of some mark and energy. They rebelled against this humble function, and claimed the right to furnish vicars in the cathedral as well as in the parish. So minor canons to take the services and choirmen to sing were appointed, and the prebendaries were free. Still, they felt that they had a duty to their cathedral. Some of the body ought always to be in charge. So an inner ring of residentiaries was appointed by the prebendaries from among themselves, varying in number but usually about six, who were bound to 'keep residence'; i.e. one at least had to be present at each service. They received a further remuneration in addition to their prebends, and in practice became the governing body of the cathedral, in the affairs of which the absentee prebendaries took little part. The residentiaries, with the dean, became, in 1836, the sole governing body, the prebendaries holding a purely honorary position. Of the old relation of this chapter to the bishop little remained save his power of visitation, often fiercely contested in the past and forgotten for several centuries, though revived in a few cases within the last few decades. This right is merely one of inquiry into the observance of the statutes, and when (as in modern times) they are duly observed the bishop has no more to say. An interesting revival, rather than survival, was the courteous desire, sometimes expressed by bishops, to consult their 'greater chapter', i.e. the residentiaries and prebendaries assembled together, on business of importance.

But the old monasteries, including the cathedral monasteries, were few in number compared with the multitude of religious houses that sprang up in England after the Conquest. For the most part they were endowed in a new way. The great primitive houses, Bury St. Edmund's, Glastonbury, Shaftesbury and the like, had received compact blocks of land around their buildings. It was no longer possible, now that England was more or less settled and prosperous, to endow monasteries with dozens of square miles in their own vicinity. Even Edward the Confessor had had to find estates for Westminster far away in Worcestershire and Gloucestershire. But the founders after the Conquest were usually more economical. They retained their land and bestowed the churches upon it on their foundation. The poorest little convent would have at least one comfortable benefice, perhaps as its sole source of income, and larger houses would count their livings by the dozen. Not that, in the aggregate, the amount of land granted to these Norman foundations was small, but that it formed a small proportion of what they needed for their maintenance. According to the thought of the age, they might take these churches and their endowments without scruple. Tithe was meant for the clergy—there is no reason to think that in England any considerable portion of it was ever devoted to other purposes—and the monks were, as a rule, taking orders. They had begun by being laymen, but amid more serious motives which prompted them to take orders was the consideration that otherwise they would be violating propriety if they took to their own use a source of income that was meant for the clergy. Hence finally, in 1311, it was ordained that they must take orders, and the only unordained monks of full age were humble and uneducated lay-brothers. But the possession of churches by monks was not only sanctioned; it was actually encouraged by the popes down to the English Hadrian IV, who died in 1159. There was reason in this preference for monks. As yet the rude farming parish priest was little regarded. His function was to do things for his people that they could not do for themselves, to provide indispensable sacraments. He was not a leader nor an influence.

On the other hand, in the great days of the rise of the religious orders the monks were in heart and soul devoted men; the austerity which was the outward expression of their spiritual life was justly reverenced and won many recruits to their ranks. They were leaders in holiness of life in a gross and barbarous age, and they became its leaders in other ways as well. But the movement of admiration was sweeping revenues needed to maintain the local clergy so swiftly into monastic channels that Hadrian felt that it needed checking. Monks (with some important exceptions) were henceforth not to be exempt from payments for the maintenance of worship in parishes where they owned lands. A more important limitation was imposed upon them, often after desperate struggles on their part, when the bishops of the twelfth and thirteenth centuries insisted that they should appoint vicars with permanent tenure and a fixed share of the income, instead of priests who were merely hired to undertake the charge. The proportions were not yet rigidly defined ; an incumbent could appeal to the bishop to increase his share, as in the established Church of Scotland he could till 1936 appeal to the courts of law. Such appeals were apt to be resented, and there is a grim story, told triumphantly by the annalist of Barnwell, how a Cambridgeshire vicar, who had dared to ask for more, died while the case was undecided, and was refused Christian burial in his own church, of which the patrons had taken possession during the vacancy, till his executors paid a heavy ransom to the offended house.

The regular clergy who occupied these houses lived all in the same methodical way. There was little difference between monks, Benedictine (though few Benedictine houses of the old kind were founded after the Conquest), Cluniac, Cistercian, or Carthusian and regular canons, Austin, Premonstratensian or Gilbertine. The last was the only order confined to England, and not great either in numbers or wealth; many of its houses were double, both for men and women, who met only in their church where they were hidden from each other by a wall of partition. All the orders had nuns who lived according to their rule and these ladies were considered to be so far clerical as to be fit recipients of tithe. Yet nunneries were much less numerous than monasteries of men. The primitive idea that the monastic life was a stern one, like that of the soldier suffering privation on active service, was so prevalent in the days when religious houses were being founded that it seemed less appropriate to spend money on houses for women than for men. The nuns seem all to have learned enough Latin to say their hours together; for the other services they employed a staff of clerks, and some of the greater houses had clergy on their foundation; at Shaftesbury there were four prebendaries. It is needless to say how magnificent the buildings of the greater monasteries for both sexes were; even the smaller had a chapel and a hall and other edifices equal to those of a college at Oxford or Cambridge. Indeed, extravagance in building was a temptation into which monks and nuns too often fell.

Monasteries needed inmates. In the days of enthusiasm, which were well over before 1300, men of mature age often joined them, but always, as it seems, the majority of their members had been trained for the calling from childhood. The little Bede had been given by his parents to the monks at seven. In his case the result was admirable; but we may doubt whether there was much enthusiasm in the case of ordinary boys, trained from childhood to take the round of services and the regular life as a matter of course. Yet the surroundings of the corporate life, its majesty, its manifold interests, financial or administrative for those of more secular mind, literary or historical for the scholars, devotional for those whose gifts lay that way, must have saved it from becoming monotonous to those who had been brought up to believe implicitly that the monastic was the best of lives and that their own was the best type of monastic life. With all its dangers, *esprit de corps* was a motive which could not be dispensed with when it was necessary to keep up numbers and maintain contentment and a good average of life and feeling. It must be said that the evidence of keen religious feeling is not usually clear, and perhaps it is better attested for humble houses than for great ones; while the conventional use of Biblical language—all monks learned the Psalter by heart as boys—was often grotesque. Education, apart from the training of novices, was no part of the proper duties of the monk, and was regarded by the more strict as a distraction from the worship to which he was pledged. It was found necessary as a means of support by many ill-endowed nunneries, which became boarding schools for young ladies, but when we hear of a grammar school supported by a monastery we must think of it as a benefit conferred by a wealthy landlord on the neighbourhood rather than as an activity of the religious body itself.

Privilege, exemption from authority, was a passion in the Middle Ages. The monasteries struggled for it, and with much success. They could not willingly submit to inspection by bishops or even by archbishops. Some of them succeeded in excluding any official visitor but a legate direct from Rome. Probably they would not have greatly gained in efficiency had they been subject to regular inspection, but they would have been more thoroughly incorporated in the national Church. The status of this mixed multitude of religious houses varied infinitely. Social considerations had their weight; parents might find it difficult to gain admission to a rich and famous monastery for a son who would be welcomed into a less conspicuous house. For within a generation or two of their foundation the first austerity and the purity of motive died down, even in the case of the Cistercians. In the competition between monastery and monastery, between Order and Order, worldly considerations became prominent. Nothing was more profitable than the funeral of some person of high estate. It meant heavy fees, handsome presents, an endowment for the maintenance of memorial services. So the Cistercians of Warden Abbey sent out men at arms to kidnap a noble corpse on its way to burial in another monastery; and when Geoffrey de Mandeville, the worst ruffian of Stephen's reign, died excommunicate in battle, the Templars took possession of his body, wrapped it in lead and stowed it away till he could obtain a posthumous absolution, whereupon they gave him a stately funeral in their church in London, to the chagrin of Geoffrey's own foundation at Saffron Walden. In fact, throughout the century which ended with the death of Henry III, we may think of the monasteries as becoming steadily less active in their religious life, and more interested in their external and political concerns. There was a stirring intellectual life even in remote houses, as is shown by the annals composed in them, and the successive historians of St. Alban's, culminating in Matthew Paris, are among the glories of England.

The heads of these houses held a conspicuous position in England. When Convocation sat, all of them were present as official members. In Parliament an increasing number received, as time went on, summons to the House of Lords, and finally their number in it was equal to that of the bishops; while the Pope from the twelfth century onwards granted one of the greater abbots after another the honour of wearing episcopal insignia. These mitred abbots were naturally in most cases those who sat as barons. Four of the chief abbesses also ranked as peers. Thus the heads of the great monasteries were of equal dignity with the bishops, and a provision had to be made for them corresponding to their position. This was done by a division of estates between the head and the house, as in the case of bishops and chapters. In some cases as much as a third of the whole revenue (or rather of the sources which furnished it) was set apart; and the relative importance of the head is seen by the pension assigned him when the house was dissolved by Henry VIII. It was often ten times as large as that of the officers next in rank to himself.

So the monasteries stood, dignified, respectable, generous to the poor, granting pensions to young clerks that they might be ordained without risk of poverty, in many ways a pride to the country and a benefit to their neighbours, and doubtless there was much sincere worship within their churches. But for two centuries and a half before their suppression Englishmen were no more disposed to increase their number than they are to add to the Livery Companies of London to-day.

The place of monks and regular canons was taken in popular affection by the friars. Christianity has had no better evidence than the life and character of St. Francis of Assisi. His entire self-surrender, his universal sympathy, his happiness in believing, have earned for him in recent days a deserved revival of love and fame. It was he who struck out the idea of a mission for God undertaken in absolute trust, without any provision for sustenance. His friars started out at his impulse to comfort the suffering and convert the heretic, the thoughtless, and the sinful, begging their bread as they went, and renouncing on principle all possession of property, not only for themselves but for their order. It was a venture of faith, and it was successful in winning back northern Italy, which was overrun with a strange Patarine doctrine that at bottom was not Christian at all. A mist of legend and poetry hangs over the words of St. Francis, his doings, and his sufferings, which neither obscures nor unduly heightens his glory. His resolve, based on St. Matthew x. 9, 10, was formed and put into execution in 1209. It found favour with the greatest of the Popes, Innocent III, who only doubted —the doubt showed his practical wisdom—whether the rejection of corporate property could be maintained. But he was over-persuaded by St. Francis, and sanctioned the rule in its full austerity. In 1219 the number of friars was so increased that they resolved to seek work outside Italy. Begging their way, strangers at first to the languages of the countries they visited, they poured over Europe, and reached England in 1224. Settling among the outcasts who dwelt in the unsanitary purlieus of the towns, they began their ministry. They had wonderful success in their appeal. It was something entirely new. The regular clergy had their vocation in offering continuous worship to God, the secular clergy were employed in sacramental service to which, it was assumed, the people would resort. But neither body had felt called to stimulate devotion, and mission preaching did not as yet fall on jaded ears. There began what may be called a national movement towards God, temporary, perhaps, but as sincere as the preaching of those penniless, bare-footed messengers of the Gospel.

But the Franciscans, or Grey Friars, were not the

first to reach England. The Dominicans, or Black Friars, came in 1221. St. Dominic, their founder, is a less attractive figure than St. Francis. A Spaniard with a passion for orthodoxy, he had flung himself into the conflict with the Albigensian heresy in Southern France, which was akin to the Patarine of Lombardy. Learning was needful for controversy, and Dominic gathered round him a body of clergy, whose task should be to refute and convince. To the heated imagination of the age miracles accompanied the preaching of Dominic, but the heretics were obstinate, and their creed was exterminated by the sword and not the tongue. Whether or not they took a leading part in encouraging massacre, the Dominicans were more conversant than any other religious body with the ways of heretics, and to them was entrusted, early in the thirteenth century, the management of the Inquisition. That grim office they long maintained; they were burning in Portugal even in the eighteenth century. But the Inquisition never took root in England. Dominic's foundation was sanctioned at Rome in 1216, but it was not till 1220 that, in imitation of the Franciscan rule, the Dominicans adopted the principle of mendicancy. With it they widened their scope, and were not less devoted and effective than the Franciscans in reviving religion and ministering to the afflicted.

The Dominicans had a businesslike organization from the first; against the will of St. Francis, who trusted to faith and impulse, a system of government was devised by his brethren and accepted by the Order even in the lifetime of the founder. The expansion had, indeed, been so rapid that a definite constitution was needed if the society were not to fall to pieces. In the case of the Franciscans there was another change of great moment. St. Francis had desired that his followers should appeal as poor men to the poor. On the other hand the Dominicans from the first felt that a part of their mission was to the educated, and had aimed at gaining a foothold in the Universities of Europe. The two Orders were working on parallel lines and often, it must be said, in rivalry, and where one led the other almost inevitably followed. The Franciscans accordingly soon entered upon University work. In England, Oxford and Cambridge were among the first settlements of both. The two struck out rival lines in theology and philosophy, and if the Dominicans can boast St. Thomas Aquinas, the official metaphysician of the Roman communion to-day, the Franciscans have had their victory in the promulgation of the Immaculate Conception in 1854, against which the Dominicans waged a conflict of centuries. In these controversies Englishmen took prominent part on either side.

These great societies found many imitators. Several more Orders of friars were founded within a few years of the Franciscans and Dominicans, all of which but two were soon forced by the Popes to amalgamate with one or other of the stronger bodies. These two were the Austin Friars and the Carmelites, who competed in England on not unequal terms with the original Orders. It was, indeed, a competition, for these unendowed bodies were all building up elaborate organizations, evangelistic and educational, without any secure source of income, and were raising churches, some of which were almost on the cathedral scale. Their activity brought the friars into hostility with the monasteries, for the gifts and the burial fees that would have gone to the adornment or to the building funds of the latter were now diverted. Even members of the royal family were buried in churches of the friars. The competition also embittered the parish clergy.

When consciences were touched, men and women wished to make confession to their new guides, who were empowered by the Pope to usurp this function of the parish priest. But the friars went successfully on their way, supported by the Pope and also by the best of the English bishops. Soon bishops and archbishops were chosen from their number. Friars sat on the throne of Canterbury in the thirteenth century. Thus strong forces, spiritual and ecclesiastical, were on their side, and they were able to organize a new thing, a comprehensive system for collecting money. Needless to say, each Order acted for itself, and in competition with the other friars as much as with the older religious forces of the country. And each Order acted for itself as a whole. Every friar belonged to the whole Order directly, and not, as was the case with the monastic Orders, through his membership of a particular house belonging to the federation, Benedictine, Cistercian, or other. Thus there was a mobility about the friars that enabled them to regard England, and indeed Christendom, as a whole, and to form and execute large plans. It seems, indeed, that in their central organization, and especially in that of the Dominicans, the idea of representation, by which the absent are bound by the vote of the present and the minority by that of the majority, was first worked out, and thence spread to the Church and the State, to Parliaments and to National Synods. Their financial system, which seems to have been similar in each of the four Orders, was that of dividing the country into districts, called 'limits', within which appointed friars travelled systematically, collecting funds for the general purposes of the society. We have travelled far from the original plan of humble emissaries begging their bread from day to day, without thought for the future or for a wider work than their own. But for the present friars were in earnest; the money was given with a good heart and was worthily spent. The 'lymytours' or 'limiters', the friars employed on this task, were familiar and welcome figures. The system had a notable effect in distributing the friars over the whole country. As the great modern banks need branches in every town of importance, so it was with the friars. The importance of the town may be estimated by the number of mendicant Orders that settled in it, mainly, no doubt, because of the scope it offered for their work, but also for business reasons. Thirteen of the chief towns had all four, nine had three, the others two or one, and there were few market towns that had none. In the villages they rarely settled; they were content to evangelize them in passing. In one more respect the friars found it necessary to tamper with their principle of poverty. They had convents attached to their churches as homes for the missioners. As time went on benefactors gave actual endowments, houses and lands, to the several convents; not, it is true, on a large scale in any case, but the aggregate revenue was not contemptible. Here was a clear breach of the rule. It was evaded by the legal fiction that the Pope was the proprietor, and allowed the friars to enjoy the income. Or else the corporation of the town was placed in the same kindly relation to the mendicants; it was made what would now be called their trustee, and this necessity of the friars played its part in developing the English law of trusts.

At the head of this great system, over parish clergy, monks, friars, laymen, stood the Pope. We have seen how a theological theory had been advanced to explain his obvious pre-eminence in western Christendom. The theory heightened his authority; it was confirmed by the feudal theory, universally accepted, that society spiritual as well as secular must have a single head,

responsible only to God. It was supported by a
succession of forgeries, perpetrated by men who
sincerely thought that they were buttressing the truth,
which for centuries were to be accepted without
demur. One of them, the Forged Decretals, has been
solemnly pronounced authentic and authoritative by
the great Pope Gregory VII. These Decretals have
played an important part in forming the law of the
Roman communion as it is to-day. The theory became
a principle, no more to be disputed than the equally
authoritative principle that the sun moves round the
earth.

The Pope, then, is irresponsible. He is bound only
by the law of nature and that of revelation, which tell
him what is right and what is wrong; and he is the
uncontrolled interpreter of both those laws. If he
abuses his trust he will go to hell; good Bishop
Grosseteste of Lincoln warned Innocent IV, by no
means a bad Pope, of the danger, and Dante in his
vision saw Popes in hell. But though men might
repine, they must not resist. This unlimited authority
is also omnipresent. Every Christian is the Pope's
parishioner: no interference on his part can be an
intrusion. And very possibly he has not only the
plenitude of authority but also the sole possession of it.
It is a tenable doctrine, and widely prevalent in the
Roman communion to-day, that bishops have no
divine origin for their authority, but enjoy it as the
Pope's delegates. Such was the postulate on which
the canon law, from about the year 1000 and at first
in Germany, was built up in the Papal interest. It
was one of two laws, the other being the civil, that were
being developed at the same time, on parallel and rival
lines and each borrowing from the other. Both were
Roman in spirit, and both despotic, each assuming the
existence of a head of mankind, supreme in his own

D

sphere. The civil law, sprung from Justinian, gained little lodgement in England, for it was repugnant to English customs and liberties. The canon law, with very similar faults and merits and a like origin, was accepted without demur as a corollary of the undisputed proposition that the Pope in the spiritual domain is supreme.

This law, partly made up of the canons of Councils, ancient or recent, partly of Papal utterances, genuine or spurious, was universal. It grew to completeness between the twelfth and fourteenth centuries, and varying as its contents did in value it was taken with equal seriousness throughout. But the law itself was not more important than its commentators. No field has been cultivated with more activity and ingenuity than was this throughout the Middle Ages. The result was the provision of a wonderful system of guidance in all the relations of life that concerned religion and conscience, when those terms were stretched as widely as possible. Marriages, wills (for the making of a will was part of the preparation for death), questions of legitimacy, the affiliation of illegitimate children, sins of every kind as distinct from crimes, and crimes themselves when committed by the clergy, were some of its topics. It concerned itself with the enforcement of promises, and punished perjury, which was a crime against God. Its rules came to be more and more elaborate, and its prohibitions more numerous. And this gave an opening for a dispensing power, superior to the law itself. You might not marry a distant cousin, but you could buy a dispensation; you must go to confession to your parish priest, but you could buy a licence to choose your own confessor. Such were typical examples of this mediaeval law, which resembled a turnpike road, with toll-gates set, not to hinder traffic, but to raise a revenue. The ultimate author of all these licences was the Pope, who was greater than the law. And undoubtedly the Popes did a great service to society by overruling and interpreting away many angularities and extravagances of their canon law, to which law, it must be said, our existing jurisprudence is deeply indebted. Now this law, being universal, was wholly applicable to England as to other countries. As Archbishop Peckham of Canterbury said, those whom Peter binds with the chain of his laws are bound in the court of the supreme and heavenly Emperor. God Himself is defined in feudal terms. It was true that long-established custom contrary to the law was regarded as locally annulling the latter; but such exceptions were few, and apart from them the English Church could not disclaim obedience. Its Convocations could, at the most, only pass by-laws, valid so far as they did not contradict the general law.

This fullness of Papal power could not always be exercised, as we shall see, but was admitted in principle from the Conquest onwards, nor would it have been disputed, as a theoretical proposition, by Edward the Confessor. The history of the English Church is largely that of an increasing submission to the claim, which steadily became more explicit and more comprehensive. For a while it was commended by the moderate use made of it and by the actual benefits which, as will appear, the Popes were able, through its exercise, to confer upon England. But in time Rome came to presume upon its admitted right: then came complaints of ever-increasing emphasis. But so long as the principle was admitted, resistance was vain. The Reformation came when this Papal right was examined, and rejected as unfounded. Then there was a new start in the religious sphere, as there was in that of natural science when Copernicus rejected the ancient astronomy.

When William I was king and Lanfranc was archbishop, the Papal claims were becoming more and more definite, and the rulers of England were, from the Papal point of view, behind the times. They held old-fashioned views concerning the appointment of bishops, which were not contested by Rome, because there was a respectability about the English Church which raised it above the level of the German, for authority over which the Popes were contending; and it is just to remember that they were fighting for decency as well as for themselves. Thus the question of the day was not at first raised in England, and Lanfranc, supported by the Conqueror, had a free hand to introduce such reforms as seemed needful. It was he who instituted rural deans in England, as officers for the local supervision of clergy and people. The latter duty, that of discovering and punishing immorality, was quite as important a part of their task as the former, which still survives, and they held regular courts at which offenders had to appear and where small wills were proved. In Lanfranc's time archdeacons also became general in the English dioceses, and soon after his day almost every county in England had its own archdeacon, while before the Conquest such officers had been few. Both these provisions for good order in the Church were after the Norman pattern, and from Normandy came all the new leaders of the English Church and the patterns that were followed in recasting its institutions, as for instance that separation between church courts and lay courts which Lanfranc and his master introduced. But though the organization of the Church had never been so perfect, it was doubtless in the main a scheme on paper. The independence of the parish clergy and the difficulties of communication were facts as stubborn as ever, and Lanfranc's machinery can never have worked efficiently.

William was strong, and his archbishop supported him, so that Papal claims, admitted in principle, were not admitted in practice. Appeals to Rome, free communication between English ecclesiastics and Rome, were kept in check; and what might have wrought a cleavage of the Church, so weakening it and strengthening the hold of Rome, was effectually prevented. York was made subordinate to Canterbury, and in due time the king and the successor of St. Augustine, working together, were to be strong enough to overthrow the mediaeval system. If York had been on a parity with Canterbury there must have been confusion of counsel and division of forces, and the Pope might have held his own. Lanfranc was unwittingly preparing for Cranmer. At the time he and William had no thought beyond that of strengthening each other. The method adopted was that of deliberate forgery. In 1072 Lanfranc produced what purported to be copies of letters written by Gregory the Great and his successors to the early archbishops of Canterbury, conveying to them privileges quite contrary to the purpose of Gregory as recorded by Bede. The originals, he said, had been lost in a recent fire, but copies had fortunately been taken, and in an uncritical age these forgeries, obviously unhistorical and teeming with anachronisms, were accepted without demur. They reduced York to a position from which neither historical truth nor unwearied protests nor unseemly brawls were able to raise that see and province, though as a compromise, finally sanctioned in 1354, York gained the style of 'Primate of England' as an approximation to the title 'Primate of all England' borne by Canterbury.

And here something must be said of forgery as an aspect of mediaeval church life. No great church, no great monastery, failed to profit by it. The temptation was urgent, for no one was likely to dispute the authenticity of the documents produced, and the mental state of the authors was not such as to be shocked, morally or intellectually, at the transgression. The men of the Middle Ages, except in strength and passions and intelligence, were schoolboys, and boys in an undisciplined school where untruthfulness, like other vices, was sanctioned by a perverted standard of honour. But beside the cases, numerous enough and especially important where the forgery was perpetrated in the interests of Rome, of wilful falsehood, there were others for which a certain excuse may be made. Half-educated people will sometimes attempt to pass off a will which they are convinced represents what was, or what ought to have been, the purpose of the testator better than the testament which he actually signed. In the same spirit many mediaeval forgeries were committed, and perhaps that of Lanfranc, though it is rather difficult to give the benefit of this excuse to a mind so highly trained as his. Yet here, as always, we must extend a certain clemency, and at the same time bear in mind that an element of weakness must be allowed for in any mediaeval examples we may be disposed to take quite seriously.

In the relation between England and the Papacy during the mediaeval period there was one advantage on the side of the former. It was often an open question who was Pope. There were strong reasons for hesitation between the rivals, and William and Lanfranc actually kept the Papacy for a while in abeyance, so far as England was concerned. And when a Pope was recognized, he had to be on his guard lest the king were offended. Hence neither of the two champions of ecclesiastical claims, Archbishops Anselm and Thomas, had the hearty support of the contemporary Popes in their conflicts with Henry I and Henry II, and in both cases the issue of the struggle was a compromise decidedly favourable to the king.

The investiture of bishops was the point of debate between Henry I and St. Anselm. The latter had received his staff, as the symbol of his office, in the traditional manner from William Rufus, and would have been ready to do homage to his successor had not a Roman council in 1099, at which he was present as an exile from the tyranny of William II, pronounced anathema against any clerk who should receive investiture of a benefice from a layman, or become his man. This was now Church law; St. Anselm felt himself bound to obey it, and left England rather than submit. Yet in 1107 he consented to a compromise by which the king abandoned investiture and received homage. This became the established custom for bishops and abbots. In the case of Thomas also, though he attained the honours of saintship by his death, substantial victory rested with the king, and the extreme claims advanced by the archbishop were dropped after his martyrdom.

But if English custom prevailed in certain respects, this did not hinder the acceptance of the canon law, and the Pope as its interpreter, as authoritative in all other matters. And the case was complicated by the uncertainty which hung over the position of Canterbury when the archbishop was also legate of the Pope. This office was at first granted as a personal favour, and lasted only during the life of the Pope who gave it, but in 1221 Archbishop Stephen Langton was made legate for life, and the office was continued to his successors. Till Cranmer dropped it in 1534, 'legate of the Apostolic see' was part of the official style of

Canterbury. In any act of authority or any decision of his court he might well seem to be exercising this legatine power rather than that of the successor of St. Augustine. And if the Pope chose, as he often did, to take some English controversy into his own hands and appoint delegates to settle it, those delegates, in that particular instance, superseded the legatine authority of the archbishop, and were also superior to him if he attempted to act as archbishop. He was ignored in the one capacity and overruled in the other, though the delegates were of lower ecclesiastical rank than his own. There was much indignation, but so long as the axiom was undisputed that the Pope is the head of Christendom, there could be no effective resistance. And when, on special occasions, legates *a latere*, plenipotentiaries of the Pope, came from Rome, there was an authority present to whom all, archbishops included, were constrained to bow in submission.

But the seeds of the downfall of the Papacy were already sown by the middle of the thirteenth century. The temptation to the Roman authorities of extending their financial resources by furnishing their officers with stipends from English and other churches was irresistible. Rome was poor, for though one of the bases of its claims was the Donation of Constantine, the local revenues were no greater than the local needs. No one had anticipated that a cosmopolitan diplomacy and a world-wide jurisdiction would arise, needing a host of educated officers who might justly claim an adequate salary. They were all clerks and so might hold benefices; they were in the service of a power which had the undisputed right to dispense them from residence. Now the English kings since Cnut had also had a staff of clerks who formed their civil service. They too needed stipends, and money was scarce in royal coffers. The benefices of the Church were an obvious resource, and if there were difficulties in forcing a high official into the throne of a bishopric, it was convenient to have Papal pressure to aid in overcoming the resistance. It was a devout imagination in cathedral chapters that they might be allowed to choose their bishop. It was sometimes promised and sometimes allowed; generally the King compelled the chapter, with or without the assistance of the Pope, to accept his nominee. There were some important occasions, especially in regard to Canterbury, when Popes ignored both King and chapter and appointed the man of their own choice in the exercise of their supreme authority; but such cases were few, and merely enhanced the value of Papal co-operation in the ordinary instances where he concurred with the king. Bishoprics were great rewards for high officials; the average clerk in the civil service had to be contented with prebends or benefices, and if he were fortunate he might secure several. But as the canon law grew more precise, attention came to be paid to pluralities. The law had no objection to these, if a licence had been bought, and the sale of the licence was as much a matter of course as in the case of a marriage without banns. And constantly in a litigious age—no society, even to-day, enjoys the excitement of litigation so much as one that is half-educated and agricultural, as was that of our forefathers—there were disputes as to the tenure of ecclesiastical preferments which could not be effectually settled without a Papal verdict, so that the business transacted for England, the most submissive of western countries and the most scrupulous as to Church property, was a never-failing source of work and income to the Roman courts. But when so much preferment was in question, why should not the Pope have his share? He was helping the King to relieve his treasury by providing his clerks with stipends; might not he claim to do as much for himself? He and his officers were clergy; the Church was cosmopolitan and he was the head of it. The temptation was too strong, and early in the thirteenth century Roman officials, who never saw England, were being paid from English endowments, cathedral and parochial. The process was simple. The head of the Church had the right to give his orders, and especially to issue them to the clergy. A bishop or an abbot was ordered to reserve the next benefice in his gift of a certain value for some Italian clerk, named or to be named; and even a custom which the English attempted to set up, that one Italian should not be immediately succeeded by another, was masterfully ignored. Clerical patrons had to submit; it was not found possible, though the attempt was made, to treat lay patrons in the same way.

Papal hold on England was strengthened when John was forced to become the man of Innocent III. John had plunged into a quarrel in which he was in the wrong; the great Pope first excommunicated him and then threatened to issue a bull depriving him of his kingdom as unworthy to reign. John submitted, and the Pope for a price gave John, not less unworthy than before, his full support. The price was that John surrendered his kingdom to the Pope, and received it back as a vassal, swearing fealty and paying tribute to his superior. What right the one had to surrender and the other to bestow the kingdom we need not inquire. In their research for sources of income the claim to feudal superiority over kingdoms was often made by the Popes. It had been attempted in vain with William I. The Pope had approved his English adventure, and construed this approval as a grant. If William had accepted a grant, he would on feudal principles have incurred the obligation of fealty to his Papal superior. But William refused to interpret the transaction in this way, and the claim was dropped. It was accepted by Henry II in the case of Ireland, of which he received the lordship (not the kingdom) from Hadrian IV; but Edward I would not consent to take, nor Robert Bruce to hold, Scotland by the same tenure. The claim to give a kingdom was easily made, and nothing was lost if nothing came of it. In the English case, however, the Popes are seen at their best. The feudal superior was bound to protect his vassal, and this was honestly done during the minority of John's son, Henry III. England was better ruled under the disinterested influence of Rome than in Henry's later life, when Pope and King demoralized each other to the grave injury of our country. But England was not long to submit to this dubious authority. It was soon ignored and the tribute remained unpaid, and finally, in 1366, was repudiated by Parliament when Pope Urban V was unwise enough to renew the demand.

Extensions of English rule both expanded and contracted the area of the English Church. Ireland, where, in the eleventh century, bishops had sought consecration from Canterbury, as a stable see and one with a definite ecclesiastical status which none in Ireland possessed, received after the English conquest an organization after the normal pattern. Though this remained in great measure a constitution on paper, it withdrew all cognizance of Irish affairs from Canterbury. The gradual annexation of Wales began soon after the Norman Conquest, and Norman bishops soon occupied the two southern sees. Wales had contained four dioceses, mutually independent and forming no part of any ecclesiastical province. The inconvenience of this had been felt before the conquest, and in the tenth and eleventh century bishops of Llandaff had been consecrated at Canterbury, and had promised obedience to their consecrators. St. David's retained its isolation till St. Anselm exerted his authority over its occupants, who were from this time onwards chosen under royal influence. The less important northern sees maintained a precarious independence during the Norman period, and it was not till Edward I's conquest of Wales that Bangor fell into its place in the province of Canterbury. Then, for the first time, Wales had a definite ecclesiastical position, though a magnificent fiction had been evolved during a struggle for the bishopric of St. David's, which provided that see with a series of metropolitans stretching back to the seventh century. In truth, there had been no Welsh Church, but only four (once five) sees in an anomalous position, loyal to the best of their ability to the general system of the Church, but with many interesting peculiarities. These in the course of the Middle Ages were levelled down, and in their worship, as well as in their organization and manner of endowment, the Welsh dioceses were assimilated to the English pattern.

It remains to say a word on the general impression that the age, which ends about 1250, leaves upon the mind. It is one of extraordinary contrasts. We find throughout very good and very bad men side by side in the high places of the Church, and neither surprised at the neighbourhood of the other. It is taken for granted that the contrast is in the natural course of things. There is no uniform standard, none of that modern respectability, which levels up, and perhaps also levels down. There is no standard because there is no uniform public opinion or steady government. On the side of good, this allows a freedom of self-development which attains to the highest points of saintliness and moral beauty. On the side of evil, this lack of governance may be compared again to the state of an ill-ordered school. We have seen it fatal to truthfulness; it encouraged also cruelty, coarseness, neglect of duty. In the field of thought no age has been more fertile in bold theories, sweeping assumptions, unlimited demands on faith. There was courage because the process was always forward; there was no criticism of the starting points. And men were the bolder in developing their ideals, and stated them in the more emphatic terms, just because they did not feel the responsibility for them that is felt by those who know that their schemes will be tested by a systematic and businesslike examination or execution. They had no need for compromise. And as it was in action and thought, so it was in personal religion. There was piety in its most attractive forms; there was gross and reckless irreverence. There was simple and intelligent belief, there was absurd superstition. But we must bear in mind that allowance, in judging persons, needs always to be made for the character of their age; and in no age have belief and morals been more obviously conditioned by the general level of civilization.

CHAPTER III

THE DECAY OF THE MEDIAEVAL SYSTEM

WE have now reached the time when, in succession to the monk and the friar, the parish priest comes to the front. Save for him the three centuries which preceded the breach between England and Rome were a time of ecclesiastical decay. In every department except the intellectual and spiritual there was progress.

But in these, the most serious aspects of life, there was no progress at all. Men continued to live by the ideas of the thirteenth century, and their scheme of thought became not only threadbare and uninteresting, like the products of a school of art or literature in its last imitative stage; it became powerless for moral influence, and ended by provoking an irresistible repugnance. Then hostility to the practice and view of life justified by the mediaeval theory of the Church led to an examination and rejection of the theory itself.

It is impossible to fix a definite date for the beginning of this process. Conspicuous and unabashed evil had been inextricably combined with the good throughout the feudal period, and expressions of resentment that bordered on rebellion may be found abundantly in writers, such as Matthew Paris in the middle of the thirteenth century, who never dreamed that a change in the system could be right, even were it possible. But the reign of Henry III is the time when abuse begins to preponderate. The King was supported by the Pope in foisting thoroughly unfit kinsmen of his own into the great sees of Canterbury and Winchester, to the public scandal, and the Pope received his reward in being encouraged to fill English preferments with Italian absentees, some of them relations of his own. Under Edward I, who established the English Parliament on its permanent footing, began a systematic limitation of the judicial powers of the Church courts and of the right of ecclesiastical bodies to accept new endowments; and his last Parliament made strong though unsuccessful protest against Papal grants of benefice. In 1305 began the really discreditable period of the Papacy, when seven successive Popes lived at Avignon, exiled from Rome or unwilling to live there. For more than seventy years (1305–77) the Popes were Frenchmen, and it was a time of hostility between

France and England. The immorality of the Papal court, though not of the Popes personally, was notorious; the extravagance was reckless, and the Popes had no scruple as to methods of raising money. The grants of benefices were no longer given as the reward of service. They were sold, and often sold more than once, so that the earlier purchaser was defrauded. And as the grants of a Pope did not bind his successor, the newcomer enjoyed the privilege of selling again all the favours of which his predecessor had disposed. Add to this that Papal justice was made as expensive as possible when cases were tried in the court of Avignon, and fees were raised to an extortionate level. Bishops and abbots who had difficulties to overcome in regard to their election were burdened with debts which often they did not live to repay, and their creditors, bankers who carried on their business at that court, exacted usurious interest contrary to the law of the Church.

What made this the more intolerable was that France was being subsidized with funds that came from England. The Popes were supporting France against England. This raised the question of alien religious houses. It had risen on a small scale in the case of Scottish monasteries. Robert Bruce and his heirs were enemies of England, and it could not be allowed that rents of English estates which Scottish monks owned should pass to a hostile land. But the case only became pressing with the French wars. Then it became clear that England could not afford to be cosmopolitan, and in spite of theory the line was drawn at the English coast. At first the alien houses saw their income pass into the king's coffers, or paid heavy sums for his licence to become denizen, i.e. purely English, neither controlled from abroad nor subsidizing the foreigner. But Church property was regarded as sacred, and soon a permanent use was made of the derelict property. English founders henceforth raised buildings, but looked to existing endowments for the maintenance of their inmates. So, for example, William of Wykeham obtained a large portion of the revenues for his great colleges at Oxford and Winchester from confiscated monastic lands. So, also, when Henry V in 1414 built his magnificent nunnery of Sion at Isleworth, its whole income was derived from the same source, as was that of Eton and King's College, Cambridge, founded by Henry VI. Thus was formed a precedent that was soon to be applied to English religious houses which might be deemed superfluous.

Meanwhile, as a reaction against the Papal claims, which were as emphatic as ever, though the power to enforce them was beginning to fail, two modes of thought were becoming prevalent in Germany which were to influence the history of the English Church. One of these was a mystical pietism for the followers of which the externals and the government of the Church had little value. It was to colour the German, and therefore also the English Reformation. The other was an imperial theory, based on theological considerations, which was a worthy rival of the Papal scheme. As exercises of mediaeval ingenuity they are equally convincing, and equally unsatisfactory to us moderns. One of the leaders in this movement of thought was an English Franciscan, William of Ockham, who lived and wrote in Germany; let it be noted that the Church was now divided against itself, and that great bodies of clerical opinion were ranged against the conventional Papal position. This imperialistic doctrine of the rights of the monarch and especially of the superiority of the sovereign, as representing the nation, to the priesthood, was to influence the English Tudors in their dealings with the Church. The fourteenth century prepared the way for the Reformation of the sixteenth.

In England itself Wyclif started a movement which had much in common with both these German phases of thought. He began as a practical reformer, giving strong expression to current discontent. But he was born in an argumentative age, and had had the scholastic training of Oxford, and he found reasons for his protest that could be construed as heresy. He was influenced by the imperialistic writers of Germany to deny the unlimited rights which were claimed by the Pope. He denied also the absolute sacredness of Church property; if it were abused, the temporal power might take it away. But he was also a deeply religious man, convinced that ecclesiastical acts are not unconditionally valid. A good man, if the Pope excommunicate him, is none the worse; indeed, if he suffer unjust excommunication, he is the better for it; Pope and cardinals cannot restore a sinner unless Divine grace be in him. The Pope is not exempt from censure and correction. Such were some of Wyclif's theses, and he had his University behind him in his demand for reform, and the reasons which he alleged to justify it. Unfortunately, the heads of the English Church were deeply interested in the maintenance of abuses, and if they condemned them they would condemn the manner of their own promotion; while the attack on them was led by a selfish body of lay noblemen, whose mouthpiece Wyclif became. There was little prospect of real reform from such an alliance, and none was accomplished.

At the height of Wyclif's struggle with the English bishops the great schism in the Papacy broke out. A contested election resulted in each candidate claiming that he had been lawfully chosen. One set up his

E

throne at Rome, and was accepted by England, Italy, Germany, Poland and the Scandinavian countries; the other reigned at Avignon and was recognized in France, Scotland, and the Spanish kingdoms. The schism broke out in 1378, and though its serious phase ended in 1409, it was not wholly healed till 1449. Europe was divided into closed compartments. Each Pope had his own dominion; even the saints of the time accepted their Pope from their nation. St. Katherine of Siena, for example, being Italian, followed the Italian Pope. Each of the two asserted that he was the only true Pope and that his rival was Antichrist. Here was an anticipation of the future. Each had his own Inquisition, at whose hands the supporters of the other need expect little mercy, though, the dominions of the two being separate, there was little actual danger; and each regarded war against a kingdom which supported the other as a Crusade. Every religious order had two organizations which repudiated each other, and England had a further reason for refusing to allow monastic rents to pass into France, where they would support an Antichrist. The schism was complete.

There was little to choose between the two dynasties. The courts of Rome and Avignon were equally corrupt and mercenary, but the Popes of the latter were of a higher type than those of the former. Yet though the faults of the Roman Pontiffs, whom England accepted, were glaring, the struggle was too keen for either party to put its worst men forward. Things only came to their worst when, under pressure from the governments and from public opinion, the cardinals on both sides had agreed to throw over their Popes and start afresh. The second election under this new system was that of John XXIII, a man as scandalous as the worst of the Renaissance Popes, who had for very

shame to be deposed in 1415.   Apart from the generally
demoralizing influence of the schism (for it is clear
that high English ecclesiastics paid the Roman court
the flattery of imitation, even though it were at a
discreet interval), the chief result in each kingdom
was that of increased exactions.   They had, in fact,
to be doubled, for each Pope had to maintain his whole
state and retinue of officials from the contributions
of half Christendom.   There had been few scruples
before; there were none now.

This further scandal of the divided Papacy led Wyclif
on to more radical thoughts.   If two Popes, why not
none?   Was a supreme and irresponsible Pope a
necessary part of the Christian system?   And was the
current theology sound?   He answered these questions
in a revolutionary sense.   The mediaeval view of the
Eucharist, upon which the power of the priesthood
rested, and which was to the general mind the most
impressive point of faith and practice, he repudiated as
idolatry, and with it the whole discipline of confession,
absolution and excommunication.   He taught that
there is but one order of the ministry, and one source
of sacred knowledge, the Bible, which every good man
can interpret for himself.   The first English Bible,
translated from the Latin Vulgate, is Wyclif's great
glory.   But the power of the English hierarchy was
too strong for him.   His doctrine was officially condemned, his University, which tried to uphold him,
was humiliated and its teachers forced to recant.
Wyclif himself was allowed to retire to his parish of
Lutterworth, where he taught unmolested, and died
peaceably in 1384.   His followers, the 'poor priests',
spread his doctrine throughout England, spiced often
with a communism that seized upon the imagination
of the peasantry, but of which Wyclif was not an
advocate.   Soon the house of Lancaster came to the

throne, weak, and largely dependent on clerical support, as the price of which a statute for the burning of heretics was enacted in 1401. It was a new thing, for heresy and its punishment had been almost unknown in the nation; but it was not such an innovation as the establishment of the Papal Inquisition would have been. There were many sufferers, and many more who recanted. Though the Lollards, as Wyclif's followers were called, gradually dwindled down to an obscure sect, they were not exterminated; trials of Lollards had not ceased when trials of Lutherans began, and undoubtedly Wyclif's teaching had prepared the way for the Reformation.

If this direct attack upon the mediaeval system failed, an official and indirect attack had a certain success. Clergy discontented with the Popes had been suggesting the assembling of a General Council since the thirteenth century. Such a Council profoundly influenced the imagination. In the Eastern Church to the present day the canons of the old Oecumenical Councils are regarded as having much the same authority as the Pope has for Roman Catholics. Councils had been an exceptional resource in great emergencies, and in the outbreak of the Great Schism it seemed that an occasion had arisen that could be provided for in no other way. There must be found an authoritative voice of Christendom that could silence the contending Popes. The personal part of the work was accomplished, but the three famous Councils of Pisa, Constance and Basel, in all of which England was represented, broke down when it came to practical reform. There was obstruction, due to vested interests; there were also national disagreements in these cosmopolitan assemblies. But their failure was an object-lesson which showed that reform could best be worked out within the single nation, and they furnished an ideal which was constantly though vainly to be before the minds of the reformers of the sixteenth century.

The new series of Popes, firmly established on their throne and hampered by no restrictions, outdid their predecessors. It is needless to do more than allude to the morals of Rome during the century which preceded Luther. Their ecclesiastical administration was cynical. Martin V, the first of the line, appointed his nephew, aged fourteen, to the Archdeaconry of Canterbury, one of the most important and lucrative offices in the English Church. Nine years later the nephew resigned it, receiving in exchange a pension for life, which seems to have been simoniacal, though the Pope could legalize it. This, like many similar transactions in regard to bishoprics as well as other benefices, was in defiance of English legislation. But successive kings, in agreement with the Popes, nullified the law; the King nominated, or allowed the Pope to nominate, and the Papal 'provision', or deed of appointment, was accepted without demur, since it coincided with the royal intention. In the fourteenth century laws of increasing stringency were passed to check Papal interference with English preferments and with English lawsuits, but with little success.

These laws were an evidence of the unpopularity of the higher clergy, which was further shown by suggestions that there should be a sweeping confiscation of Church property. But this tide of feeling even among the orthodox, rendered more formidable as it was by the popularity of novel doctrines, only caused the bishops to cling more closely to the Popes. They felt that the existing system must stand or fall as a whole, and were conscious of the value of the impressive doctrine of Papal supremacy for the maintenance of the established order. The occupation of bishoprics by the younger sons of the great families, often promoted with little regard to their fitness and sometimes at an uncanonical age, was a complaisance of the Popes which became common towards the end of the Middle Ages. Quite thirty bishops of this class held office during the fourteenth and fifteenth centuries. Though alien bishops were not very numerous, three in succession held Worcester from 1497 to 1535; their appropriate successor was Hugh Latimer. For one year (1521–22) the future Pope Clement VII, with whom Henry VIII subsequently quarrelled, held Worcester as an unconsecrated 'administrator'; i.e. the income was transmitted to Italy on his behalf. Meanwhile the general respect for the office was disappearing. In the same two centuries an archbishop and three bishops perished at the hand of mobs, and Henry IV, allied as he was with the hierarchy, had no scruple about beheading an archbishop of York for treason. Three aliens, who were promptly dispossessed, held English bishoprics at the time of Henry VIII's breach with the Pope.

But if bishops were unpopular, their chief officers were detested. The most conspicuous duty of the archdeacon was disciplinary. It was his business not only to prove wills, with fees and duties from which he made large profit, but to correct sins. This latter function made his office one with cure of souls. It could be executed by deputy, and always was so when the archdeacon was an absentee; archdeaconries were favourite gifts of the Popes to their Italian friends and servants. In theory the purpose of their courts was the correction of sins; offenders had therefore to be sought out for their good. Hence the employment of the summoner, one of the ugliest figures of the age. He passed through the district in advance of his master, seeking whom he might report for slander, incontinence or other faults. His opportunities were obvious; a bribe would silence him if a man of any means were the culprit. For humbler folk there was public trial in church, with a shocking sentence of being scourged so many times round the walls of the church, which was regularly commuted for some small fine, such as sixpence. The Scotland of Burns offers a very faint survival of this mediaeval abuse.

The monks were a decaying body, in discipline, in numbers, and in prosperity. When there were few openings in life for young men, it was usual for families of moderate estate to give a younger son to a monastery. It was a favour to the house, which could not dispense with recruits, and it relieved the family of a burden. Enthusiasm was unlikely in a monastery so replenished; the life was a career, like another, and relaxation was enjoyed in such ways as it could be had. With nunneries the case was the same, save that it was quite common to pay the house a lump sum to take charge of the daughter. The life was normally respectable, though there were scandals, but the houses were isolated and neither occasional visitations by bishops or legates nor by heads of other houses within the Order could do much to remedy the stagnation. One example of the growth of ease may suffice. The Cistercian Order reached England early in the twelfth century. A feature of its very stern rule was that meat or fat might not be cooked or eaten within the walls. Two centuries later the breach of this law was so general that it even received Papal sanction. But the written rule remained, and the monks now built a second kitchen and a second dining-hall under other names that it might be observed in the letter. By this innocent subterfuge they could still say that in their kitchen and refectory meat and fat were unknown.

Though there were a few new foundations, largely endowed, as we have seen, with the property of alien priories, the number of monasteries was steadily diminishing for more than a century before the general Dissolution, and also the number of inmates in those which survived.   Openings in the world had increased, and willingness to enter 'religion' diminished.   If the great houses were at a loss to find inmates, the smaller were half, and more than half, empty, and even in the fifteenth century some were quite derelict.   The wisdom of founders led them to prefer colleges at Oxford and Cambridge as the objects of their generosity, and the weaker monasteries were a welcome resource. So Bishop Waynflete, the founder of Magdalen at Oxford, in 1458 got Papal permission to annex Selborne Priory, an almost empty house of Austin Canons, and in 1496 Bishop Alcock turned the Benedictine Nunnery of St. Radegund at Cambridge, which had fallen into ill repute, into Jesus College.   The process went on more boldly as time advanced.   The Lady Margaret obtained several religious houses for her two colleges at Cambridge; Cardinal Wolsey got leave to suppress no fewer than twenty-two for his foundation at Oxford, and Henry VIII followed in the same path.   Though he dissipated Wolsey's original endowment, he re-endowed Christ Church with monastic lands and churches, and the great Abbey of St. Mary at York was the chief source from which he endowed Trinity College, Cambridge.   The cause of the decay of the religious houses was in part financial. Some of the greatest, especially St. Alban's, had never been adequately endowed.   They had great expenses, and were expected to maintain a lavish hospitality. This was possible till the friars attracted the public mind and drew off the large, though irregular, income from gifts and burials by which they had been in part supported. Furthermore, founders and their representatives—in the case of the great monasteries almost always the Crown, either through foundation or through the extinction or forfeiture of the founder's family—had a claim upon the houses. This took the form of saddling them with pensions called 'corrodies', often for worn-out servants but also for officials of the highest rank. For instance, Sir Thomas More, Lord Chancellor, had a pension out of Glastonbury. This strain upon their finances, and perhaps also an unbusinesslike administration, forced the monasteries to be hard landlords. They could not afford to be generous. No incident is commoner in their later history than riots of their tenantry against them, often very destructive, and sternly suppressed. There was, then, little sympathy felt for them; their state was not unlike that of the unreformed Colleges in Oxford and Cambridge before the days of Royal Commissions. There was also discontent within. In England as on the Continent the authors of the Reformation were for the most part regular clergy, monks or friars. The Elizabethan Archbishop Whitgift said that he learned his principles from his uncle, Abbot of Wellow in Lincolnshire, under whom he began his education. In fact, what earnestness there was in the convents must have largely taken the form of inward revolt before the Dissolution, and there is no reason to doubt that a multitude of the less earnest were quite willing, when the suppression came, to take their pension and be free. There was, however, one small and austere Order, that of the Carthusians, which, when the time of trial came, was unanimously ready to suffer rather than deny its allegiance to Rome.

The friars were in even a worse case than the monks. Their need of money demoralized them, and there is no reason to doubt that Chaucer's picture of the wandering 'lymytours' does them substantial justice. It must be at any time difficult for a professional collector, whose success is inevitably measured in terms of money, to preserve delicacy of feeling; it is no wonder that in a coarse and credulous age impudence and imposture were prevalent in the class, which in its turn infected the remainder of the Order. But here again there was one small body resolved at any cost to be true to its convictions. The Franciscans, the most enthusiastic and sometimes the least balanced of the Mendicants, were early divided between those who observed and those who neglected the founder's strict rule of poverty. The latter became dominant, and comfortable houses, maintained to some extent by dubious means, became their dwelling instead of the rude lodging of their predecessors. A more conspicuous departure from the rule was the wearing of shoes, in contravention of St. Matthew, x. 10. All this raised protests within the Order, and the struggle ended in the recognition in 1414 of the 'Observant' Franciscans as an Order distinct from the original or 'Conventual' body. The Observants had some few establishments in England, and in their last days resisted Henry VIII as bravely as the Carthusians were doing.

In the age of decay, when bishops, monks and friars were in the main losing the respect of the nation, and when as an even worse symptom, the 'pardoners', or hawkers of indulgences, were pervading England, the parish clergy first stand forth as the best representatives of religion. We cannot say this of the secular clergy as a whole. The bishops ordained far too many priests, and multitudes lived precarious and often disorderly lives, with little more employment than that of singing funeral masses for fourpence after some rich man's death. Great importance was attached to the multiplication of these services; wills provide for a thousand masses to be said on one day, or for chaplains to be hired to say a mass each every day for a year; or else permanent chantries were endowed without pastoral duty, though fairly often the chaplain chose to teach boys, or was even expected to do so. But chantry priests, like the multitude attached to cathedral or collegiate or monastic churches —the larger monasteries had many small endowments for the purpose—were not a very satisfactory class. The wealth lavished by the laity on their parish churches in the fourteenth and fifteenth centuries, the period of Perpendicular architecture, shows whither the affection of the people had turned. Great churches were built, especially in the eastern counties, which bore no more relation to the number of parishioners than did the cathedrals to the population of little mediaeval towns. All the arts of the time were employed in sculpture and painting, in woodwork and alabaster and in coloured windows. The splendour of the result, of which little but the architecture remains to-day, marks the esteem cherished for the parish priest. When men honoured monks and friars they built for them; now it was for the clergy, who would not have been so favoured had they not in great measure been such as Chaucer's 'poor parson of a town'. We need not take the poverty too strictly: there were good livings as well as bad, then as now. The point to be marked is that the parson is the religious leader of his parish, and no longer the mere performer of religious rites. He has taken the place which he still retains. No wonder that the rich men of the parish prefer to adorn their church rather than some religious house elsewhere, and that guilds in which all classes join are formed to worship together and to contribute towards the splendour of its service.

It was natural also that, in an age when the representative idea was fixed in the public mind, this general support of the parish church should be supervised by representative churchwardens. They first appear in the fourteenth century, and though the funds they administered were for the most part voluntary gifts, there are early instances of those compulsory church rates which became universal under the Tudors.

The social position of the parish clergy varied greatly. A comfortable rectory in the gift of a landlord was likely to be occupied by one of his family; and it has been noted how, as rectories fell into the hands of monasteries and were converted into vicarages, the names of the new incumbents are apt to show a lowering of their status. But now for the first time on a large scale there appears a disposition on the part of the laity to remedy this impoverishment of the livings by fresh endowments. It was the more necessary because the monasteries persisted in their policy of appropriation. Many vicarages were instituted even in the sixteenth century, on the eve of the Dissolution, and had not the process been abruptly stopped it would doubtless have become as complete as it was in France before the Revolution, where the parish clergy were almost all the humblest of peasants, and theirs a career upon which no man of position or education would dream of entering. In fine, we may say that in spite of many absentees and licensed pluralists, the parish clergy of England in the generations before the Reformation were the salt of the English Church.

The last feature of these two centuries that need be mentioned is another proof of a heightened regard for the secular clergy. It is the foundation of Collegiate churches, of which some, such as Manchester and Windsor, were on a magnificent scale, though the great foundation of Henry VI is an instance of economical endowment. Broad lands in Dorset which had belonged since Alfred's time to Shaftesbury were diverted to this new purpose; and it may fairly be said that the nuns of Shaftesbury could afford to lose them. But, unhappily, these Collegiate churches, though to a less degree in England than in Scotland, were often supported out of rectorial tithes, and so were another cause of poverty to the working clergy. And the canonries in them, as in cathedral churches, were very apt to be held in plurality by absentees. Hence they were not an unmixed blessing to the Church, as the Colleges founded in the Universities, the teaching staff of which in practice, if not quite always in theory, consisted of secular clergy, undoubtedly were. But the choice by founders of these two types of benefaction show that the seculars were now finally superior to the regular clergy in the general regard.

CHAPTER IV

THE BEGINNING OF THE REFORMATION

EARLY in the sixteenth century it was becoming clear that the Middle Age was passing away. New forces and new thoughts were becoming dominant, and nowhere would they work greater change than in the Church of England. But its structure was to survive the shock. Constitutionally it was made up of an indefinite number of bodies and individuals, holding certain rights and properties to which corresponding duties were attached. The Church itself had no property whatever, either directly owned or held in trust on its behalf. But it had a true unity imperfectly expressed in its organization, of which unity it was very conscious. It also had a strong and venerable position in the State. Its bishops and many of its abbots sat as peers, and formed the majority of the Upper House; it was an estate of the realm, taxing itself and enjoying considerable powers of legislation; and, what was equally important for the future, its rights of property were rooted in the land and therefore were defended by the Common Law. Patronage had grown out of the lordship of land, glebe was land, tithe was produced by land. All rights and wrongs concerning these had to be discussed in the King's courts, and the immemorial tendency of those courts was to protect the freeholder.

The Church was also national in the sense that the public conscience required every man to adhere to it and attend its worship. Heresy was a sin for which few thought that death was too severe a penalty. But, being national, it was still bound to the Papacy by the theory, as yet undisputed, of the right relation of national churches to the Pope. Yet the very fact that the Churches of England, and of all the great nations of the West, now regarded themselves as national was evidence that a new relation must be devised between them and the centre at Rome. Now, Rome being what Rome was in the age of the Renaissance, reform was imperative and the initiative had to be taken by the lay power, for the Popes and their courts were quite content to remain as they were. So in Spain there was a thorough and deeply conservative reform imposed upon the national Church by the monarchs, after which they insisted, sternly though respectfully, that Rome should reform itself. The purification of Rome was the work of Spanish kings, using their dominions in Italy as a menace which the Popes dared not disregard. France proceeded on a different line. Nowhere had the Popes been more interfering; now they were treated not as an integral part of the French system, but as an alien power with whom an agreement, a *concordat*, may be made. The King allows the Pope certain privileges, in return for which he stipulates that there shall be no meddling from Rome with the ecclesiastical matters which the State reserves for itself. Control over the Pope and a treaty with him were both of them devices that might be regarded as consistent with the mediaeval system, though they were hard to reconcile with the full Papal claims. Was a third policy, that of ignoring the Pope and yet maintaining mediaeval doctrine and discipline, any less consistent with the past? Could a kingdom be catholic on those terms? Henry VIII was to make the experiment.

But in Germany a more drastic procedure had been adopted. There Christianity showed both in better and in worse aspects than in England. There was a true and widespread personal religion, both among those who joined and those who resisted the movement of Luther. On the other hand, nowhere were scandals more flagrant among the higher clergy, and that with Papal encouragement. An astonishing pluralist was Albert of Brandenburg, to one of whose dioceses Luther belonged. At twenty-three, having none but secular interests and those of a gross kind, he received the archbishopric of Magdeburg and a bishopric as well; next year he received in addition the greatest German see, that of Mainz, paying heavily for the sanction of Pope Leo X. The transaction was concealed under the form of the purchase of an indulgence issued by the Pope; i.e. the Pope, in return for a lump sum, allowed Albert to take his chance of making a profit by retailing copies of the indulgence among the people of his two provinces. The trade was carried out by 'pardoners', such as Chaucer has described, who employed the methods of the cheapjack to pass off their wares. The object of the Pope was to pay for the rebuilding of St. Peter's; it cost him and his successors Northern Europe, for it excited Luther's protest, the burning of the Papal bull on October 31, 1517.

That Germany was ripe for change is clear from his instantaneous and peaceful success. Within a few years prince after prince had disowned the Pope, and established a new church on Luther's lines in his dominions, and the example was quickly followed by the Scandinavian kingdoms. The problem of government for these new churches was a grave one. It was hopeless to look to Rome, which to all appearance was incorrigible. A generation was to pass before any serious attempt should be made at reform in that quarter. The only other resource was the princes, and Germany was already familiar with reasoning which gave supreme authority to the prince. To the princes, then, Luther appealed, and they were not loth to listen. As the highest authority, they were entitled to annex the domains of bishops and abbots, and they justified their claim by establishing, after Luther's plan, an orderly system of parochial preachers, over whom they set 'superintendents', sometimes called 'bishops', the head of the whole local system being the prince. The German Emperor down to the present century claimed, as King of Prussia, the *summepiskopat* over his communion in his dominions. Luther's sole interest was in the encouragement of personal religion and of doctrines which he thought were true. The Church, to his mind, existed merely for these purposes; he was indifferent to the Church as such, and to history. He might easily have secured continuity with the past, for bishops were among his supporters, but he did not think it worth while. But he was resolute for the thorough execution of his plan. The prince, he taught, who had the Divine authority to establish a church had also the right to use the sword to enforce obedience. No one might preach without official licence, and no one abstain from attendance at the lawful worship.

Such was the system established throughout Northern Germany, and advocated in books which found their way to England, and were eagerly read in the English Universities. It was the doctrinal opposition to Rome that attracted men there; but statesmen could not be blind to the fact that a system of church government based on the right of the Sovereign was working successfully a few hours from our shores. Henry was in doctrine a convinced mediaevalist; but a strife which was discreditable to all engaged in it save the unfortunate Queen Katherine drew him into a position which could not be reconciled with any recognition of the Pope's authority. If the King was to have his way, it could only be by asserting that England was self-contained as a religious community and complete in itself. If it were so, if the centre of English religious life lay within the circumference and not outside it at Rome, who was the human head of the Church? It could be no one but the King, and the justification of the claim could be only that imperial line of argument which had been worked out in the fourteenth century and was now being displayed in action on German soil.

But for many centuries the Popes had enjoyed in practice a supreme authority over the English Church, as over the rest of their communion. That authority might be justified in two ways; either as a matter of principle, the Pope being taken, as he claimed to be, for the representative of God on earth; or else as

F

being the exercise of a number of rights conceded to him by overt or tacit sanction of the Sovereign. Henry took the latter line, and argued that what had been granted could be resumed. It was resumed, first by the submission of the clergy in 1532, confirmed by Parliament in 1534, and then by the Act of Supremacy, also in 1534. These documents do not profess to make the King 'the only supreme head in earth of the Church of England', but provide that he shall be 'taken, accepted and reputed' as such, and therefore arrange for a new system, legislative and judicial, that shall fill the gap made by the withdrawal of his powers from the Pope. It was a new thing to part from Rome; but the royal supremacy, now emphasized, was as old as English kingship. The King had always been supreme over all his subjects, clergy and laity, and over all their affairs.

Neither Henry nor his subjects dreamed that a new Church was being established. The old Church, its clergy, its rites and revenues went on as before. Into the last a grave inroad was made when by surrender, attainder and parliamentary suppression the monasteries disappeared. Yet it must be remembered that the monks were steadily encroaching on the parish clergy, and that with the suppression the turning of comfortable rectories into poor vicarages came to an end. But a multitude of clergy who had been paid to sing services in monastic churches now lost their work, and the number of the unemployed was also increased by all the regulars who had to eke out their little pensions by such clerical work as they could get. This superfluity of clergy had important effects. It emptied the Universities by deterring young men from an overcrowded calling, and it ensured that for a generation there should be a majority of clergy convinced of the older views.

All this, however, did not affect the character of the Church. A Church, or a nation in its religious aspect, does not lose its identity when it changes some of its views, any more than a philosopher or a politician. And it must be borne in mind that the change was not in the object, but in some of the accessories and mechanisms of religion. Nor must it be forgotten that the position of the Pope had been rendered doubtful by the conciliar movement. It had been widely taught, and not authoritatively denied, that a Council is superior to the Pope. The world might have been quite wrong in its subservience to him, and a General Council might any day reconstruct the faith and practice of Christendom. It was no assault on an uncontested authority when Luther and the other reformers appealed to a future Council to decide between them and the Pope, and when Bonner, the future Marian bishop, appealed to the same tribunal against Henry's excommunication by Rome. The supreme government of the Church had become an open question, and conservative churchmen might feel justified in abstaining from recognition of a disputed claim.

After the severance from the Pope the affairs of the Church were carried on with increased decorum. The day of magnificent pluralists was over; there was no second Wolsey, with his Renaissance morals. The doctrine inculcated in official publications and enforced by criminal proceedings under Acts of Parliament was quite traditional, and if there were some fluctuations of policy they came to little. Two bishops who held the views that were coming in from Germany were forced to resign their sees; one of them was Latimer. Deprivation and burning were often inflicted on teachers of the new doctrines. Most of the leaders in the future Marian reaction were men who came

to the front under Henry. Gardiner, Bonner and
Tunstall were among his bishops. The better government of the Church was provided for by six new sees,
one of which, Westminster, was unfortunately suppressed under Edward VI; but they were so poorly
endowed that it is unjust to charge their occupants
with pluralism for holding other preferment with them.
Till the nineteenth century it was a necessity. We can
hardly regard the circulation of an English Bible and
the introduction of an English litany into the churches
as revolutionary measures. The nearest approach to
the future made by Henry (save the great suppression,
with which some proceedings of the Emperor Charles V,
Papalist as he was, are comparable) was the destruction
of shrines and images, as objects of superstition. But
this was in the spirit of the Renaissance as much as
in that of the Reformation; with the spread of the
temper in which Erasmus had visited Canterbury
pilgrimages would soon have ceased. So the great
experiment of conservative churchmanship without
the Pope was consistently and mercilessly carried out
during Henry's life. There was intellectual sincerity
on his part; moral and spiritual sincerity also in the
better men who co-operated with him. But the
experiment was doomed to failure, for the world had
not been standing still. Luther's doctrine had spread
in England, in spite of burnings, and not Luther's
doctrine only.

Strange exaggerations of teaching had arisen in the
ferment of thought that he had awakened; but however the new preachers might vary, they were at one
in their hatred of Rome, which stood in their eyes for
the denial of Christianity. From the Low Countries
such doctrine passed into England, and though it had
to be propagated in secret it did not fail to spread.
But Switzerland was to be a more potent influence.

Zwingli completed his drastic reformation of Zurich before 1525. Unlike Luther, he wished a complete breach with the past; for him nothing that Scripture did not command was binding on a Christian man, and he made it his business to strip off everything in worship and belief that was not in the strictest sense essential. He was an intellectualist, with a clear, uncompromising mind, eager to rob religion, especially on the sacramental side, of all that was mysterious. His teaching, bold and modern and as it seemed progressive, was to have considerable influence in England, and Bullinger, his successor, was to be an oracle for Elizabethan bishops. The Reformation on Zwinglian lines not only spread through the greater part of Switzerland; it also encroached on Lutheran territory, and was the one form of revolt from Rome in France and the Netherlands. Thus England was separated by a screen of 'Reformed' lands, as they were technically styled, from the States which were 'Protestant' in the strict sense, i.e. Lutheran.

The cleavage between Lutheran and Zwinglian was profound, and in 1529 became impassable. It was one not only in specific doctrine, especially of the Eucharist, but in spirit. It was conceivable that the Lutherans might revert to a purified and conciliatory central Church; for Zwinglians it was impossible. Soon the Lutherans came to regard themselves as in a certain sense allied with Rome against the latter, and when English reformers came to look at the great debate through Zwinglian eyes they too were alienated from Lutheranism. Finally Calvin arose to give its final shape to 'Reformed' thought. His 'Institutes', the textbook of his school, appeared in 1536, eleven years before the death of Henry VIII, and at once made its influence felt, especially through its great doctrine of Predestination, as opposed to Free Grace, but also as the most cogent and logical system of non-Roman theology. In 1541 Calvin made himself master of Geneva, which became the model community in the eyes of the Reformed.

The Continental movement was thus triumphant and its leaders were rejoicing in the prospect of further conquests while the English Church was still holding firm to the traditional system, somewhat simplified and purged, and above all made strictly national. In the last respect it agreed with all the successful movements abroad. Each of them held that the State for religious purposes is a whole; all its members must hold the same faith, follow the same worship and discipline, and be protected from error. This principle had been taken over from the mediaeval system, and was enforced not only as sound in itself, but because internal unity was a necessary protection against Rome. There was no mercy for those who held that religion is a private matter, and that men should combine for worship with those who agree with them. That seemed disintegration of the State. But heresy was also as repugnant to Reformers as to Romanists. The former had fewer temptations and opportunities than the latter, but a fair number of Anabaptists suffered in England, and Zwingli approved when the men of Zurich drowned one of them in their lake, while an occasional Unitarian was burnt in England from Edward VI to James I, after the example set by Calvin in the case of Servetus.

Even in Henry's days the leaven had been working in England. Cranmer was peculiarly susceptible to foreign influences. Loyal as he was to his master's ideal, his mental explanation of the system was first almost Lutheran, and then almost Zwinglian. He had all the admiration of the younger men for the adventurous theology of the Continent, and as soon as the

King was dead he was busily welcoming its representatives to England. They came from all quarters, from Italy and Poland as well as from Germany, and were of all shades of doctrine. Bucer, a Lutheran who was almost Zwinglian, became Regius Professor of Divinity at Cambridge, and Peter Martyr, an Italian of like views, received the same office at Oxford; both had been friars. Bucer soon died, but Peter Martyr lived to fly from England at Mary's accession, and to exercise a strong influence over the English exiles in Germany. These and the other visitors under Edward found English thinkers in a receptive mood, with little respect for the old theology and little confidence in themselves. It may be said that till Hooker arose, they made no contribution to the guidance of their own Church; as in later days Germany has been regarded as a model in science and in war, so then were Germany and Switzerland in Christian doctrine. Not only was weight given to the counsel of the foreigners resident in England; matters of difficulty were referred to the leaders abroad, and their words of reproof or encouragement awaited with deference. The more the revolting churches appreciated each other, the more did they emphasize their common repugnance to what was characteristic of Rome. This centred on the doctrine of the Eucharist. Though they differed as to a Real Presence, all denied a propitiatory sacrifice, and all were emphatic in asserting that the ancient service was an antichristian rite. None exceeded some of the English reformers, such as Ridley, and even Cranmer in his last phase, in the vehemence with which they denounced the Mass. By the end of Edward VI's reign it seemed that the English Church, unchanged in structure and continuous in existence, was pledging itself to the truth of the more radical Swiss doctrines.

But in two matters of the utmost importance the Swiss friends were allowed little influence. The hereditary constitution of the Church, both in relation to the State and in the manner of ordination of its ministers, was not assimilated to the Continental models, and the genius of Cranmer—the word is not too strong—endowed England with an order of service adapted from the old Sarum use and rendered into perfect English. There was foreign influence, but in this case it was chiefly Lutheran, and the outcome was a very conservative Book of Common Prayer, which was to satisfy the great majority of those who held with Henry's policy, while it was not intolerable to the foreign reformers, and to those in England who followed their counsel. It was only the extreme men in both directions who were to reject it.

The whole result was a phase of the Church in which it ranked as one of a number equally orthodox, and equally opposed to Rome. The leaders abroad recognized it and its ministry, though they thought its reformation inferior to their own because it was less thorough. It was valid, but not perfect. On the other hand, the English were apt to be somewhat apologetic in their tone. They had done their best, and if the result was below the achievement of Zurich, still it was sufficient. But it was ominous for the future that even in the second half of Edward's reign, when an extreme policy was in favour under the influence of Warwick, John Knox refused to be Bishop of Rochester, and the equally austere John Hooper, the future martyr, had to be imprisoned for several weeks before he would accept the see of Gloucester. In the eyes of such men the English Church was tainted by its continuity of usage, and it was sin, or almost sin, to acquiesce.

But such views were never to be dominant. What

might have befallen had Edward's reign been longer than six years, it is vain to conjecture. Towards the end the pace of change was swift. The reign of Edward VI had begun with a moderate policy. Change was inevitable, but communion in both kinds and leave for the clergy to marry, both of which were demanded by Convocation and granted by Parliament, were conciliatory measures desired by many opponents of the Reformation on the Continent. The same may be said of the first Act of Uniformity and the first Prayer Book of Edward VI. These aimed at unity in worship, did not affect belief, and concerned only the clergy. But soon the conservative bishops suffered deprivation, and their successors pressed onward. London and the Eastern Counties were with them, the North and West were hostile. Ridley and his Dean introduced the table, set in the middle of the chancel, into St. Paul's in place of the altar, and such an example was widely followed. But a stronger force than episcopal control or example was that of local feeling. Government in the sixteenth century had no machinery of its own. It depended on the magistrates of the counties; if they were of the reforming spirit, any excess was winked at; if they were conservative, the old services were protected. And the freehold position of the clergy was as strong as ever. It was difficult to deprive them in any case, and the machinery of the episcopal courts was out of gear. So, in spite of legislation, there was much diversity, and it cannot have been lessened when, after three years of the first Prayer Book, the second was sanctioned in 1552. Though in substance it was the same and it retained its literary merit, the changes made aimed at more perfect conformity with Continental standards. But this service-book and the Act of Uniformity which imposed it had little more than a year of life, and the

English Church was never again so nearly to merge itself in the European federation opposed to Rome.

The leaders of the Church were supporters of the singularly corrupt and unpopular government of the later years of Edward VI, and the Archbishop and Bishop Ridley of London were compromised by their share in the vain attempt to continue it with Lady Jane Grey as Queen. When Mary ascended the throne amid public sympathy, their fall was inevitable. Mary at first proceeded cautiously. For more than a year she held, and used, her statutory powers as Supreme Head of the Church, and when, in the first session of her first Parliament, the whole of her brother's ecclesiastical legislation was repealed, she stepped into her father's exact position. The bishops deprived under Edward were restored, and they were men who had sanctioned Henry's action by holding their office under him; some indeed had been his agents in attempting to procure the divorce from Rome. But Gardiner and Bonner had learned that their former attitude was no longer tenable. In face of the strong spirit of reform in England they could not hold their own without external support, which must come from Rome and Spain. Amid fears and doubts and warnings from Philip of Spain the restoration of the Roman obedience was carried through by Mary and Pole, the Papal legate, who was soon to succeed Cranmer at Canterbury. In November 1554, seventeen months after Edward's death, England was solemnly reconciled to Rome, the headship was abolished, and all the Acts against heresy were revived.

Then, in February 1555, began the martyrdoms; the exodus, which was equally important, had preceded them. While several bishops and a multitude of the leading clergy, among them most of those whom Elizabeth was to make bishops, fled to Germany or

Switzerland, Cranmer and Ridley, whose danger was greatest, rejected the opportunity of flight. The deaths, in less than four years, of the archbishop, of four bishops, and of others who at the lowest estimate were near 300 in number, had a decisive effect in alienating England from the Church in whose behalf these things were done. Happily the reign of Mary was brief. Towards its end it was embittered not only by her own ill-health but also by strife with Rome. The half-crazy Neapolitan, Paul IV, went to war with Philip, who was King of Naples as well as of Spain, over South Italian politics, and therefore Mary also was technically his enemy. Paul punished her by depriving Archbishop Pole of his legateship, and taunting him—Pole was a moderate supporter of reform within his communion and especially at its head—with suspected heresy. All this hardened Mary's heart, and persecution grew steadily fiercer. Revolution must soon have come had not death anticipated it.

CHAPTER V

THE REIGN OF ELIZABETH

ELIZABETH mounted the throne amid grave difficulties. As the daughter of Anne Boleyn she represented revolt from Rome, and the nation expected her to reverse the whole disastrous policy of her sister, of which Romanism and persecution had been a part. But, thanks to ill-guided policy, England was weak and dependent on Spain for protection, and the jealous care of Philip lest his sister-in-law's dominions should fall under French control was her best safeguard in the early years of her reign. Papal excommunication, and a Papal summons to the faithful to assist a French invasion for the suppression of heresy, might have been fatal. But Philip kept the Popes under restraint, and was himself a counterpoise to France. Elizabeth was not put under the ban of Rome till she had reigned nearly twelve years, and then she and England could stand unsupported. Secular policy, aiming at the balance of power, had hindered the fighting out of the religious issue, and had given time for those who had accepted Henry's system to reconcile themselves to it once more after their brief trial of Rome under Mary.

It was, then, under the shelter of Spain that the English Church was settled on permanent lines. But the settlement was not easy. Convocation was opposed to change; most of the dignified clergy had been appointed under Mary, the proctors, elected under the eye of her bishops, were men of her school, and the episcopate as a body was hostile to change. Elizabeth, however, had her way, and restored the system which her sister had abolished. No place could be found in it for the persecutors; they had to suffer ejection, but there was no such retaliation as had disgraced Mary's reign. This mercy was, indeed, a necessary result of the theory on which Elizabeth's advisers acted. It was taken for granted that the evicted had been lawful occupants of their posts till they vacated them by non-compliance with the law. There was no charge of heresy against them, and their treatment was, considering the spirit of the age, very gentle. But though the higher clergy were removed, those in the parishes were hardly affected. Only some 200 were deprived; the rest, even those of Marian ordination, assumed, or resumed, without demur, the position as it had been under Henry, only twelve years before, and each year that passed must have made them feel the better justified in holding it.

But these quiet souls were not to control the future. That was to be the lot of the exiles who flocked back to England on the death of Mary. There was one improvement on the time of Edward; the foreigners stayed at home. It is true that they still exerted their influence. English reformers consulted them, reporting progress made and asking their approval, but this was in private; the public government of the national Church was in English hands. But over this government there were keen struggles which had already broken out during the exile. It had, in fact, become clear before the return that the aims of two parties among the exiles were incompatible. The one may conveniently be called the Anglican, the other the Puritan. There was no serious difference between them in doctrine. It was common ground to the two that in the Divine order there must be a national Church, with a coercive government, to which all members of the nation must belong, joining in its worship and accepting its doctrine. It was also common ground that England, under such a sovereign as Elizabeth, had such a Church, orthodox and non-Roman. The point of difference was as to the manner of its government. The Anglicans were content with the moderate reform of Edward VI, and were ready to worship according to his Prayer Book. They did not think that the retention of ancient words and vestments (or at any rate of the surplice) was a compromise with error. Their courteous reception by foreign hosts at Frankfort and elsewhere showed that these too regarded the survivals as harmless; and this sanction weighed with them, for they had no thought of unchurching their German and Swiss friends. On the other side, the Puritans were for a complete and

conspicuous difference from Rome. This struggle
had already begun, and was most furious at Frankfort,
where Cox, the future bishop of Ely, led the Anglicans,
and John Knox with Foxe, the future author of the
Book of Martyrs, their opponents. Foxe, whose great
work was to be a potent influence against Rome, to
the end of his days was in trouble about his surplice.
Knox effected a reformation to his mind in Scotland.
Neither party was, or could on principle be, tolerant;
each was aiming at entire control of the Church. It
happened that the Anglicans had the first opportunity
of suppressing the rival school.

Matthew Parker, Elizabeth's first archbishop, was a
reformer of moderate temper, who had lived in con-
cealment during Mary's reign, but had not left
England. His interest was largely in the historical
aspect of the English Church. With the past as
connected with Rome he had little sympathy; he took
his share, like Cranmer, in the Eucharistic controversy,
and judged Rome by what he regarded as its errors of
doctrine. But he laid stress on the continuity of the
working system of the Church; it was an evidence that
the Church, in spite of change, was still itself. Hence
he magnified his office, on which Henry had conferred
greater powers than earlier archbishops had enjoyed.
All the special licences which the Pope had hitherto
granted were now, so far as they continued legal, to be
granted by the archbishop of Canterbury; for instance,
licences to hold benefices in plurality were, and are,
granted by him alone, even in the province of York.
Hence abuses, which lingered even into the nineteenth
century, for when the whole constitution of the Church
was in peril, it had seemed dangerous to Parker to
touch even its weaker points. The English Church,
then, was to manifest its continuity by retaining its
constitutional position and the immemorial ordination

of its ministry, and by a worship and an attire of its clergy that should remind its members of the past; but it was also to be a reformed church, recognizing its sister churches abroad and recognized by them. But Elizabeth and Parker had no mind that it should lose its identity and be merged in a new reformed cosmopolitan system.

Yet if they and the majority of quiet people were content, there was a strong body both of clergy and laity otherwise minded. In exile they had grown familiar with churches where repudiation of anything that could remind men that once they had been in communion with Rome had been raised to a principle. To such men a rochet, a surplice, a collect from the Sarum use were marks of Antichrist, and it seemed their duty to rescue their Church from such defilement. At first this party fought for externals. Parker insisted on obedience, and rather than obey, grave elderly men of high position, the Dean of Christ Church among them, resigned office. There was much indignation. Some of the bishops were doubtful of the wisdom of such rigour; they sympathized with the sufferers, shielded the rebellious, and were only kept from joining in their resistance to the law by the expostulations of the more moderate foreign reformers, who feared lest disunion might lead to a recovery of England by Rome. It was a more serious matter that the leading laity were often of the same mind. What they wanted was a strong national union against Rome, and they were ready to condone or encourage irregularities in men who were the extremest and most logical opponents of the Pope and his ways.

Thus the task of Parker and his colleagues was very hard. They had no clear fighting position like that of their opponents; their attitude seemed to be one of compromise and could not be set forth with rhetorical effect. And, unfortunately for them, though the Queen wished them to succeed she foresaw that they might fail, and was determined not to share the unpopularity they incurred. It was at their own risk that they proceeded, and they had little success in the parishes. For bishops' courts had lost coercive power; bishops might, and did, hold visitations, but these only informed them of the state of affairs and gave them no force to correct the mischief. The Queen withheld as yet the support which as 'Supreme Governor'—she had chosen this instead of 'Supreme Head' as the title to be given her in the Act of Uniformity passed at the beginning of her reign—she had power to give.

It was no wonder that Puritanism grew apace, and that its advocates expected soon to be masters of the national Church. Parker was sure that in his hands it was the old Church. They would have denied that proposition, but they were convinced that under their charge it would be the same orthodox, national Church of which Parker for the present had control. Soon they had a machinery to propose for its amendment. The Scottish revolution of 1559 was followed by the legislation of 1560, which made Scotland in Puritan eyes a pattern kingdom. It combined parity of ministers with an organized system fitted for a nation. Geneva had been too small to furnish an object-lesson in that respect. Parity of ministers became from 1570, when the Cambridge Professor Cartwright came to the front, the real issue, and it was, unlike the quarrel about vestments, a controversy worthy of serious men. It had been mooted in print as early as 1561, and services of the Genevan type had been held in secret in London in 1565. In the country, under the protection and with the connivance of local magistrates they may well have been held earlier. But when the Genevan ideal of worship was combined with the principle, asserted to be scriptural and permanently binding, of the equality of ministers, the danger to the existing system became pressing. The new scheme was that of a regular hierarchy of ministers, those of each neighbourhood being organized in a *classis* and deriving their authority from their recognition by it. Above the *classis*, which might correspond to an arch-deaconry, were to be wider assemblies culminating in a national one, which in its turn, if the system were perfected, would send representatives to the supreme authority, a cosmopolitan general council of the reformed Churches. It was a bold plan, but it had actually been set in action, up to the national assembly, in Scotland, and the promoters were confident of the same success in England. But there came to be a grave schism in the Puritan ranks. There were Independents among them as well as Presbyterians. These Independents also accepted the idea of a national Church and an endowed ministry, but in their eyes there was to be no representative system controlling the independence of the parish clergy. The Church was to be a federation of parishes, with no power in it higher than the individual minister and the officers chosen by his congregation; so would the little churches of the New Testament be repro-duced. This was the doctrine, as it seems, of Robert Browne, the father of English Independency. He was not a Separatist, who would have only voluntary 'gathered churches'. When he fell into trouble in England and fled to Scotland he was promptly imprisoned, for the doctrine of Independency seemed anarchical to Presbyterians. Both of these types of Puritans were ready to accept the national Church, if it were reformed to their mind. They asserted that it would not be a new but only an improved Church if they had their way; and even now, imperfectly

G

reformed as it was, they allowed that there was no actual sin in attending the services of its stricter clergy. The Independent Church established in New England was of this type. Its members regarded themselves as belonging to the Church of England. They had a parochial system, and in Massachusetts a state position till 1834. But the bitterness of oppression drove some Elizabethans into actual Separatism. They would make no compromise. For them attendance at church because it was the national Church was a compliance with Antichrist, even though the doctrine taught in it were their own. Such men were Barrowists rather than Brownists, taking their lead and their popular name from one of the three Separatists who suffered death under Elizabeth.

The first and most formidable attack was that of the Presbyterians, headed by Cartwright and Travers, the opponent of Hooker. On the other side the leader came to be Whitgift, Archbishop of Canterbury. He was a strong Calvinist in doctrine, and held the Pope to be Antichrist, but though for him episcopacy was unessential he was a strong upholder of discipline. The English Church was organized on episcopal lines, and therefore good Christians should accept that system, which was more seemly than any other, and had an immemorial history behind it. When he came into office he found discipline relaxed through the half-hearted policy of his predecessor Grindal, who died in 1583. Grindal had looked only at the personal goodness of the Presbtyerians, and his charitable interpretation of their motives made him blind to their revolutionary scheme of setting up an administration that should undermine and abolish the existing polity of the Church. In his day Elizabeth had come to be alarmed at the divisions within the Church, and was resolved no longer to be neutral. She would cast the strength of her government on the side of the established order, secure uniformity as a first step towards unity of feeling, and forbid the propagation, in print or by speech, of dissident views. Grindal failed her, and for the last years of his life was suspended from his office of archbishop.

Whitgift, supported on the intellectual side by Hooker and on the practical by Bancroft, Bishop of London, who was to succeed him as archbishop, laid the foundations of success. Hooker, one of the greatest of English thinkers and the first writer of classical English prose, combated the whole Puritan position. The Bible, he taught, is not the sole code of rules for Christians, nor are they bound mechanically to reproduce the church government described in it; and in fact, the government of the first ages was not Presbyterian. The Church is a society, and societies, like individuals, have their right and place in the Providential order. They grow, and shape themselves. The visible Church in general, and the English Church in particular, have shaped themselves on episcopal lines; episcopacy is 'a sacred regiment, ordained of God'. They were right to do so, and their members must be loyal to their constitution. As things have turned out, there are reformed Churches which have no bishops to ordain their clergy. Historical necessity has made them what they are, and Englishmen need not criticize them. Such was Hooker's contribution to the cause; Bancroft, keen and pugnacious, made it his business to detect and thwart the Presbyterian plan, and did not recoil from methods that a modern politician would deem undignified. For he had made up his mind that argument, the method of Hooker, was useless; nothing but rigour could succeed.

The enemy was formidable. The passionate sympathy

of the English people for the suffering Protestants
of France and the Netherlands, who were treated like
the Albigenses of old, the methods and the doctrines
on the Roman side being exactly those of the thirteenth
century, excited admiration for the Calvinist belief
which sustained the heroes of the struggle.   Calvinist
doctrine led on to Calvinist discipline, which attracted
the younger men in the Universities as a scheme of
organization.   The course of the Presbyterian movement has, in fact, a strong resemblance to that of the
Oxford Movement of the last century.   Both began
among fellows of colleges at the Universities who made
converts among the influential laity.   In both movements parishes in which the doctrine might be taught
were obtained by the presentation of lay patrons, and
both causes, in face of opposition in the parishes, and
especially from the bishops, ended by winning a
public for themselves.

The first great Puritan movement rose swiftly, and
was swiftly suppressed.   In 1584 a petition to Parliament was presented, praying for relief from conformity.
In the same year the Presbyterian scheme was put
into action, the Puritan clergy assembling in local
classes, and regarding them, and not their bishops, as
the true authority over them.   Two years later there
was actually, though secretly, a national assembly held
at Cambridge, and in 1587 in London.   Meanwhile
the Queen and Parliament were bombarded with
petitions, and a secret press flooded the country with
pamphlets by 'Martin Marprelate', in which the
existing system of the Church was denounced with an
Elizabethan breadth of humour which lessens the
impression of sincerity.   Bishops were described as a
'swinish rabble', and Whitgift as 'the Canterbury
Caiaphas'.   Strict measures were taken, Bancroft
being among those most active in tracing out the

leaders in the campaign, and in 1592 the attempt came to an end and the *classes* broke up.

The bishops had won because they were now backed up by the High Commission. This was a royal court, established by authority of Parliament, with extensive and indefinite powers to right evils that the ordinary courts could not touch. It came, bishops being among its members, to exercise a wide jurisdiction in ecclesiastical affairs. The bishops' own courts had ceased to have any coercive power; and the High Commission was a prompt and efficient substitute. It was very effective in saving for the clergy tithes or other revenues of which the tyranny of patrons, or corrupt bargains for the sacrifice of income into which they had entered with their presentees, were often depriving them. For the spirit of encroachment which Henry VIII had engendered, and which was not extinct in Elizabeth, had penetrated into the parishes, and Bancroft did a lasting service to the Church in bringing such extortions to an end. But that court was especially effective in keeping the clergy, whether they were simply indifferent or animated by Roman or Puritan spirit, up to the Anglican mark. It could override the protection furnished to such offenders by the local magistrates, and insist by fine and imprisonment and even (though rarely) by deprivation on at least a minimum of rubrical order being observed. Thus the Church in the later years of Elizabeth had a powerful, if not quite ecclesiastical, instrument of coercion. Discussion was suppressed, but at any rate, in the compulsory quiet that followed, men grew to be accustomed to the appointed order of worship, and custom bred affection for it. There is no doubt that, while there was deep disaffection under the surface, that devotion to the Prayer Book and the Anglican system which marked the churchmen of the Stuart age was also gaining ground. Now for the first time there came to be a strong volume of opinion in favour of the Church as being not merely comparatively but absolutely good, and worthy of the best loyalty of its members.

CHAPTER VI

THE STUARTS

In the later years of Elizabeth the English Church had found itself. The strong conservative feeling that survived from the days of Henry and Mary had found satisfaction in the Prayer Book. The Popes, induced by political motives to postpone their condemnation of the Queen and Church for twelve years, had contributed to this result. The average Englishman inevitably felt that a Church which Rome hesitated so long to denounce could not be very bad, to say the worst. And when the Papal condemnation coincided, obviously not by chance, with Spanish hostility, his loyalty was engaged on the national side. If he took the Roman side, he was an agent, perhaps a victim deliberately chosen for sacrifice, in an international struggle. Comparatively few were ready to welcome the danger, either to themselves or to their country. Happily there was soon a schism among those who took the risk. The secular clergy, unlike the Jesuits, knew how to combine loyalty to their Church with loyalty to their nation. They and their followers managed to make a secret agreement, largely through Bancroft, with the government. The Jesuits, seeing that they were the weaker party, changed their tone, and gradually the Roman Catholics accepted the position of a peaceful, tolerated communion, whom their opponents, with some discreditable lapses, ceased to suspect and persecute.

The great majority of the conservatives became in time acclimatized to their English worship. The same was the case with most of the Puritans. In the later years of Elizabeth they abandoned their hope of reconstructing the Church, and acquiesced in conformity. They found that in the existing system there was nothing intolerable to their conscience, provided (as was the case) that they were allowed to interpret it in their own way. They adopted clerical dress in church and abroad, and they followed, often not very completely, the rubrics of the Prayer Book. Thus habit was formed, and though patrons of Puritan mind presented clergy of the same temper, conformity in a loose sense became general. This was promoted by the steady pressure of the High Commission, for though comparatively few were actually summoned, none of the disobedient was sure of safety. But, though custom often grew into preference for the established order, the cases were numerous in which there was a mere submission. Such men felt that the system fell far short of their ideal, but they submitted, for at least it gave them a position in which they could exercise their ministry, and the opportunity of working for a change.

The moment for the change seemed to have come with the death of Elizabeth. James I came to England from that pattern of Presbyterian order, the kingdom of Scotland. Puritans who were yearning for such discipline in their own land did not dream that the King was escaping with joy from a system for which he had conceived a deep repugnance. He meant to enjoy to the full his constitutional rights in regard to the English Church, as Henry and Elizabeth had done, and his experience of Scottish ministers with their oligarchical, rather than democratic, authority had made him enamoured of episcopacy. 'No bishop, no king', was his maxim from the first.   In their ignorance of all this the Puritans met him with a great petition, which, so they claimed, represented a strong public opinion, and James, wishing to know how the land lay, gratified them by ordering the Hampton Court Conference to be held in 1604.   It was a false step, for it was a public recognition of the party he meant to suppress.   Elizabeth would never have put the Puritan leaders into open equality with her bishops; it was an advertisement for them of the utmost value.   From the Conference itself they derived cold comfort.   All their wishes, ranging from the desire to be relieved from the vestments up to the demand for the power of excommunication for presbyters and the rest of the full Scottish system, were rejected, not too courteously. Nor were they more successful in saddling the Church with the stern doctrine of predestination which Whitgift had formulated in vain in the Lambeth Articles of 1595.   It was true that James accepted this, the approved Protestant orthodoxy of the day, and in 1619 was to send English divines to sit among the delegates of the foreign Calvinist churches at the Synod of Dort, where the opposite doctrine was condemned; but happily it has never been the express doctrine of the English Church, though it has been widely held within it till the nineteenth century.   The Puritans had to retire from the Conference utterly disappointed.   Its practical results were the completion of the Church Catechism by the questions and answers on the Sacraments, and the Authorized Version of the Bible, work on which was at once begun.   These were uncontroversial topics on which both parties were agreed.

The chief contrast between the policy of James and

that of Elizabeth was that the former trusted the heads of the Church. He allowed self-government, and especially he sanctioned the passing of a code of laws for the Church, which hitherto had lived since Henry's day under a confused system, partly statutory, partly drawn from canons which retained their force as not being contrary to legislation, partly consisting of royal or episcopal injunctions and advertisements, the coercive authority of which was doubtful. James decided to remedy this confusion. But there was the grave practical difficulty that from Henry VIII onwards the official doctrine had been that in ecclesiastical matters, affecting laity as well as clergy, the legislative power lay with the Convocations (i.e. in practice with that of Canterbury) subject only to the royal assent. Canons so confirmed were as valid as Acts of Parliament which had received the same assent. Parliament, it had been held, had no rights over the Church, and the Crown had successfully resisted its intrusion into that domain. But the Crown was now weaker, and public opinion, which found voice in Parliament, was stronger than ever before. Hence the canons of 1604, the work of Convocation and Crown, were a hazardous experiment. It is true that they were studiously moderate. For instance a 'decent table', to stand anywhere in the church, satisfied their requirements, and would satisfy any Puritan; but there was an irritating number of canons to which penalties, often necessarily, were attached, and the whole code by its claim to universal authority seemed a defiance of Parliament. It was to be a cause of friction down to the Civil War, for Puritan representatives in Parliament were to be constantly objecting to the canons either in principle or in detail, and hostile resolutions, which the Crown would ignore, were frequently to be passed.

If Parliament would not acquiesce, it was at first a still more serious matter that the law courts prevented the administration of the new code. There had always been jealousy in England between the different courts, and under James the Common Law judges were able to assume, much as the French judges did in the eighteenth century, a rather unreal attitude as champions of liberty. For there was a question as to the legality of the High Commission's powers, and clever lawyers induced the judges in many instances to prohibit the execution of the orders of the Commission. There was another reason beyond the constitutional. The lawyers had an instinctive respect for freehold rights, and when the High Commission was seen to be attacking the 'parson's freehold' they were at once in arms. Here again the comparative weakness of the new dynasty was doing its work. Even a Coke might not have been so bold against the wishes of Elizabeth. Very often the clergy menaced were simply indolent or scandalous, but the procedure against them was exactly that which was employed against an obstinate Puritan, and all alike were protected by the prohibitions of the Common Law. Before long, it was true, a private compromise between the judges and Bancroft, now archbishop, was reached, by which protection was withdrawn from flagrant offenders. But the 'freehold' had been vindicated; and it must be borne in mind that all penal action by bishops to-day has the express sanction of Acts of Parliament. The immediate result of the activity of the High Commission in enforcing the new canons was that some three hundred clergy were suspended or otherwise punished, and perhaps fifty deprived. There was general submission after that, but a resentment the keener that it was concealed; and the Puritan patrons continued to present men of their school to

vacant livings, who conformed but whose sympathies
were Presbyterian.

Meanwhile the Church was making notable advances. On both sides, among those who approved
and those who submitted, there was an increase of
efficiency. The incomes of the clergy were better
paid, and their social position, at least among the
beneficed, was maintained. Churches were beautified,
and there are few generations to which we owe more
in this respect than the one which gave us our Jacobean
oak-work. In spite of deep cleavage the clergy had
found a *modus vivendi*, and if things had remained as
they were permanent peace might have ensued, one
school or the other quietly dying out. For as yet
there was a broad common ground. Bancroft recognized the foreign reformed Churches as of the same
nature as his own, and had no scruples about the
holding of English preferments by men ordained in
them. And what seemed the greatest triumph of the
day, the falling into line of the Scottish Church with
the English in the matter of bishops, was an admission
of the same principle. It was recognized on either
side that bishops, being superintendents over ministers,
must be chosen from among ministers. When three
bishops for Scotland were consecrated in 1610, they
were men in Presbyterian orders, and thus the English
bishops expressed a judgement of their own in favour
of that ministry. Those Scottish bishops never
confirmed, used no order of service save that of Knox,
wore Genevan gowns; they were in practice only
permanent presidents of synods, who as such conferred
ordination. It was an object lesson in compromise
to which appeal was to be made more than once,
though unsuccessfully, in the coming troubles. For
the present it worked well enough in Scotland, and
Abbot, who had been an efficient agent in reconciling

the Scots to the measure, had his reward in being made Archbishop on Bancroft's death. Under him there was no likelihood of innovation.

But beneath the calm surface of conformity there was much agitation. Hostility to Rome was as violent as ever among the conforming Puritans. But Rome was growing fashionable, especially among great ladies of the Court. The slight suspicion of danger only made the intrigue more exciting. And the royal family itself was suspected. No other royal house of the first rank adhered to the Reformation; princes must marry their equals, and marriages involved danger to the national communion. The wife of James I was a secret Romanist, and the alternatives in the case of his son were a Spanish and a French princess. The latter, when she came, was not only a protection to English members of her Church but also an active proselytizer. No wonder that Puritans and old-fashioned English churchmen grew suspicious, and scented danger in everything that might suggest Rome, and not least in the canons of 1604, which were largely, and reasonably, drawn from ancient or mediaeval sources.

For a new spirit was coming over the more churchly element in our communion. It was a great age of learning, when scholars ranked as high as scientific discoverers do to-day. One chief field for discovery was in the literature of the early Christian centuries. Englishmen took an honourable place in these pursuits, and England attracted great scholars, such as Casaubon, from abroad. They were no Romanists, but members of reformed Churches who came here because the English Church resembled the ancient as none other in Christendom did. Thus Englishmen came to be proud of their Church. Its very peculiarities were a cause of satisfaction; no longer was Geneva or Zurich or Edinburgh the pattern, and the shortcomings of the English reformation a matter of regret. And this new feeling was augmented by a knowledge of the existing Greek Church. The Turkish East was a chief seat of English trade, and the merchants supported chaplains, among whom were some of our best clergy and best scholars. They collected manuscripts to enrich English libraries, and brought back not only books but news of a venerable and stately Church that preserved its immemorial doctrine and worship, and yet was thoroughly hostile to Rome. Thus a new standard was set, and that interest in patristic orthodoxy which since then has been dominant among English theologians was awakened.

Our divines were eager to make the most of the points in common between England and the orthodox East. Conspicuous among these was episcopacy, which therefore gained a new importance. A gulf was opened between the English and the other reformed Churches; the difference between them seemed to be one in kind, not in degree. And when emphasis was laid on episcopacy, Rome seemed nearer. This, indeed, was a concession that had to be made in the effort to retain the waverers among the upper classes. They were tempted by Rome, and it would have merely alienated them to assert that there was no goodness in the Roman communion. There obviously was, and it was sound controversial method to make the most of it in order to point out that England had all Rome's merits, and had even more. Here again episcopacy was a matter to be emphasized. It became not merely an evidence of continuity but a part of the essential constitution of the Church and a ground for its claim to the allegiance of its members. It passed from history into theology, and it was the most conspicuous difference between the reformed Churches abroad and those of England and Scotland; for in the latter, though minimized and half-concealed, there was now an episcopate.

That the two schools of thought should continue side by side in one Church was growing increasingly difficult. It was made impossible by the Anglicans. Their very merits alienated the other party. A new sense of the beauty of religion and of its accessories was being developed. Poets such as George Herbert and Vaughan were casting a halo round the worship of the Church, and it was being commended by the holiness of men like Bishop Andrewes. But it was all ecclesiastical, and it irritated the unecclesiastical Puritan mind, for it seemed, quite wrongly, to be specifically Roman in origin and tendency. And it was connected, unjustly but naturally, with the extreme theory of the Divine right of the King that was being preached by reckless men. This was, as we have seen, a mediaeval doctrine devised as an antidote to the Divine right of the Pope. It was now being used to justify royal absolutism, in faithful imitation of that effusive loyalty which the Greek Fathers had shown to a Constantine or a Theodosius. Charles I had been ruling and collecting taxes without a Parliament for eleven years when the collapse came which forced him to summon the Long Parliament and endure the Civil War; and all the time the leaders of the Church, headed by Archbishop Laud, had been ostentatiously approving his course. Juxon, the Bishop of London, had actually, as Lord Treasurer, been one of his most responsible ministers during the last and worst part of the period. The Church seemed to be compromised beyond repair by this association, and this at a time when political and religious issues were inextricably intertwined. But not only had the Church supported a policy, which, if it failed, must be as

disastrous to the bishops as to the king. It had also
continued to use to the utmost that dubiously legal
instrument, the High Commission. Always in what
he deemed the interests of righteousness, but often
with masterful unwisdom, Laud had employed it in
ways most distasteful to the Puritan mind. He could
do so with a clear conscience, for Divine right overruled for him constitutional considerations; but the
objects at which he aimed were as repugnant to the
Puritans as was his method to the men of the Parliament. Nothing could have saved him, and the Church
as he knew it, save success, and he and his party failed.
Yet even on the brink of disaster he had foreseen no
danger and learned no prudence. A new code of
canons, amplifying and strengthening the former,
passed Convocation and received the royal assent in
1640; it professed to bind a laity which was on the
brink of rebellion.

But the teaching of this school was as offensive to
the Puritans as its practice. Men like Laud and
Andrewes were free from the crude dogmatism of the
age. Though they were resolved to have worship
uniform, they were willing to leave many speculative
issues open, and this want of definiteness was regarded
as indifference to truth. Yet their worst offence was
that they denied the great Calvinist doctrine of Predestination. They were Arminians, as the school was
called after the Dutch teacher who had been condemned
at Dort. That Christ died for all, and that all might
profit by His death, was a belief that was not regarded
as even respectable, for till Arminius propagated it
among the Calvinists of Holland, it had only been
taught since the Reformation by some Anabaptists and
some early Unitarians. To teach it was to defy the
great doctor St. Augustine, to whom the Puritans
paid undoubting homage. The Anglican school did

no greater service to English Christianity than this challenge to prevalent belief; and in the long run, as we shall see, their doctrine was to prevail, though the struggle was to last into the nineteenth century.

Arminian, tolerant in doctrine, martinet in discipline, committed to a false constitutional theory that was to fail disastrously in practice, Laud had no suspicion that his King's support would be the ruin of his cause, and his very virtues would cause his downfall. When the Long Parliament defied the King, it was the religious grievance that sharpened the political strife, and every effort Laud had made to encourage reverence counted as a provocation. He was the most unpopular man in England, and was punished early in 1643 by the Parliament's abolition of episcopacy, and by his own imprisonment and subsequent execution. It would be utterly unjust to estimate his character by his weaknesses. On the scaffold (Jan. 10, 1645), he asserted that 'he had always lived in the Protestant Church of England', thus disclaiming both Calvinism and Romanism.

But the Parliament had to build a new structure in the place of what they had overthrown. They called to their assistance the famous Westminster Assembly, which met in July 1643. Then it appeared how far the school of Laud was from predominance. From every county in England came grave, elderly, learned men, episcopally ordained under Elizabeth or James, beneficed clergy who had conformed for years to the Prayer Book and worn their surplice. They regarded themselves as conservatives, maintainers of the Elizabethan tradition, loyal to the canons of 1604. Their patrons had been the country gentry, in many cases men who were to side with the King in his conflict with Parliament, though a number of great noblemen and landlords such as Manchester, Essex and Bedford, were on the Puritan side and had also appointed men of the Westminster type. These divines, now that they were free to mould the Church after their will, showed that their bent was Presbyterian. Their conformity had been no more than tolerance. The English Church had been a true Church, to whose rules they had submitted without sin, but it had been sadly imperfect. Now they would amend it after the pattern of 'the best reformed churches'. The result of their labours was a Confession of Faith, part of a 'covenanted uniformity in religion betwixt the churches of Christ in the kingdoms of Scotland, England and Ireland'. That Confession, drawn up by English beneficed clergymen with a few Scottish assessors, is still authoritative for the Church of Scotland. But they did more than frame a creed. They shaped a Presbyterian discipline for our Church, which was made law by an ordinance of the Long Parliament in 1646. But Englishmen flinched from the prospect of ministers ruling them with the rod of excommunication, and the Presbyterian system, which the need of Scottish military aid against the King had alone induced the majority of Parliament to accept, was never effectively established save in London and the neighbourhood of Manchester. The dream of a Presbyterian England, cherished for more than seventy years, was finally dissipated, and the party was soon reduced to ineffectual efforts to make a compromise with churchmen, by which bishops should survive, but be shorn of almost all their powers.

The place which the Presbyterians lost was taken by the Independents, whom the army supported. We have seen that within the Puritan ranks there had soon appeared a school which held that Scripture justified no larger unit than the single congregation. They shared the general belief that a nation ought to have a

H

national Church, and this, according to them, ought to consist of an aggregate of mutually independent churches. The nation had a right to insist that its members should attend public worship; therefore there should be a sufficiency of churches, and a stipend for those who conducted their services. But beside this outer circle of attendants there ought to be an inner circle round the minister, who formed the 'Church' in their technical sense. This should co-opt its members and control the administration of its affairs. Neither the State nor any other authority ought to have power to command the 'Church' to admit a member, or to coerce any one into becoming a member of the 'Church'. This very indefinite system was set up under the Commonwealth, and worked better than might have been expected.

There were, of course, many vacancies to be filled. The royalists were the first to create them. From the western counties in their possession they ejected, as a military precaution, the clergy who sympathized with the Parliament. These fled with their families to London, where a 'Committee for plundered ministers' was established for their relief. A cheap and obvious method was that of retaliation. Clergy of royalist and churchlike tendencies were driven from their homes in the eastern counties, and the refugees installed in their place. As the control of Parliament extended, the process was continued, though without the same excuse. From livings that were worthy of the name all the clergy save such as were of Puritan sympathies were ejected; in the poor livings which no one desired many strong Anglicans were permitted to remain. It will be found that the income of the parishes where, according to tradition, the Prayer Book was used throughout the troubles, is almost always pitiful. It is a vulgar error that uneducated and scandalous men were numerous among the Puritan intruders. The truth is that there were plenty of young men, educated at the Universities and ordained by the bishops, but holding the principles of the Westminster Assembly, who were either unbeneficed or holding poor livings which they were quite ready to leave for better ones. The system of patronage remained, and patrons were unlikely to present men inferior to their Anglican predecessors; and there was careful administration of the great mass of episcopal and capitular patronage which, with that of the Crown and of royalists incapacitated from exercising their rights, was now at the disposal of the government. There was strict examination by 'Triers', ministers appointed to test the qualification of candidates, and in every county there was a Committee of Religion, consisting of county gentlemen who exercised the powers of institution and supervision that had belonged to the bishop.

Under the Independent régime of the Commonwealth the clergyman who could once obtain a living and keep on good terms with his parishioners was under no higher control. In practice, even if not in principle, he was an Independent. The Law Courts protected his freehold and enforced the payment of his tithes; the one thing that was not done was to compel attendance at his church and to give him the monopoly of preaching in his parish. The strange and not exaggerated stories that we read of the religion of the time belong to the private adventurers who formed congregations where the doctrine of the parish church disagreed with their own; such eccentrics were rare among the legal occupants of the benefices.

Among these were a considerable number of strict Anglicans, several of whom, such as Bull and Lake, afterwards became bishops. The Triers were only

concerned with the piety, blameless life and competent
knowledge of candidates, and the county committee
made no difficulty in admitting them to benefices if
they could obtain a presentation. They would, in
fact, have had their remedy at law if they had been
rejected. The only limitation imposed was that they
might not read the service from the Prayer Book. As
part of the policy of suppressing 'Popery and Prelacy',
this was forbidden. But they were not forbidden to
recite the services by heart, and this we know was done;
while, as we have seen, a number of undesirable
livings were left in the hands of their original occupants,
who ventured to read the prayers, secure in the knowledge that no one envied their position. But where the
Anglicans were themselves intruders, daring to use
the Prayer Book in parishes occupied by Puritans, little
mercy was shown them. Their meetings were broken
up by the military, and minister and congregation
haled to prison. Yet such outrages commonly
occurred when the government was alarmed by
rumours of royalist plotting, and there were intervals
of comparative safety.

These distresses ended with the Restoration, when
trouble began for the other side, who had, for their
part, recklessly provoked retaliation. With the return
of the King all existing rights came again into force,
and among them those of the beneficed clergy, who
had clearly been ejected by unconstitutional measures.
All who survived returned to their homes, and there
was a much larger ejection than ensued two years
later. Yet the latter event created a greater emotion.
The Act of Uniformity of 1660 ordered that all the
intruding ministers who were relieved by the death of
their predecessors from the necessity of vacating their
livings should, if they were not in Holy Orders, remedy
that defect within two years, and that the use of the

Prayer Book should be compulsory from the same date. The term for obedience was fixed on St. Bartholomew's Day, 1662. The former requirement did not cause great difficulty. Before the troubles unordained ministers were almost unknown. No scruples had been felt by men of Puritan mind over this point. From the leaders who had sat in the Westminster Assembly downwards, they had regarded Anglican ordination as a rite which might conscientiously be undergone, since it was the rule of the reformed national Church. Only men of about forty years of age or less can have been affected by this rule, for they had entered on their ministry since the deprivation of bishops; there is evidence that many used the interval to obtain ordination, which the bishops, in the interest of peace, were glad to confer. Many also had been secretly ordained under the Commonwealth by bishops who were living in privacy, but they were men who had looked forward to the restoration of the old order. The real hardship was in the numerous cases of elderly men who, like the Westminster divines, had been ordained and used the Prayer Book in their earlier days, then for a number of years had laid it aside, doubtless with pleasure, and now were bidden to resume its use. Conscience might allow them to do so, but self-respect would not. Yet their choice was difficult. They might choose the humiliation of adopting a mode of worship, the inferiority of which they had long been proclaiming by their doctrine and practice, and incur the reproach of subordinating conscience to income. Or they might choose to sacrifice their position, though in so doing they were leaving the service of a Church which would still be, in their eyes, a true national Church, and were abandoning the work to which, as they believed, they had been called to devote their lives. We must equally respect those who decided in either way. Among those who refused to conform were some who may be called, without paradox, higher churchmen than others who preferred the opposite course. The number who went out is traditionally stated at 2000, of whom a very large proportion were lawfully ordained. The truth cannot be stated as yet, and guesses are profitless. The materials are in existence for discovering the facts, and doubtless in time the comprehensive study of parish registers and other documents will bring them out. But it is probable that the whole number of Presbyterians, Independents who were not Separatists, and Separatists of various types—a certain number of Baptists had been installed in livings—who resigned their posts on St. Bartholomew's Day, was a good deal less than is commonly assumed.

This severity was impolitic. If the self-esteem of good men, who were often fathers of their parishes, had been sheltered by permission to retain for their life the use to which they had accustomed their parishioners, a great secession would have been avoided. They were willing by retaining their posts to give their approval to the activity in the parishes around them of men of the Anglican school; in the most emphatic manner they would have been showing that they regarded them as brethren in the ministry of the same Church. They would have shown that in their judgement the differences were unessential, and it would have been easy to require their successors to fall into line with the general discipline. Divergence would not have been raised into a matter of principle.

But the passions of the Restoration Parliament were too heated for wise counsel. The members were set upon a violent reaction, and since they were resolved to maintain the political attitude of the Long Parliament the only sphere in which they could revert to the model of the past was the ecclesiastical. They outdid Laud in severity, and the severity was the work neither of King nor bishops but of the Commons, who faithfully expressed what was for the time the mind of the nation. The tyranny of the Commonwealth, its government by major-generals, its failure in all respects save foreign policy, had exasperated the English people, and Charles I, who had truly been a martyr for his Church, since he could have turned the scale and recovered his position had he been willing to abandon it in favour of either the Presbyterian or the Independent system, had risen to be a popular hero. He had lost his life because he would not sacrifice his Church, and men were quite in earnest when they dedicated churches to 'King Charles the Martyr'. And with enthusiasm for the King went eager acceptance of his archbishop's teaching. It was a Laudian generation. That scheme of faith, Arminian and Anglo-Catholic, was inculcated with massive learning and commended by graceful and romantic piety. But the force of events and the tendencies of thought were to counteract this revival and bring it for a while to nothing.

The policy of persecution was awakening a spirit of resistance, and a 'dissenting interest', which politicians turned to account, was being formed. It was a sign of the times when Charles II in 1672 issued his Declaration of Indulgence, permitting dissenting worship, and releasing those who had broken the law, and among them John Bunyan, who had spent almost twelve years in prison. Though Parliament insisted on its rights and compelled him to withdraw the Indulgence, things could be no longer as they had been. Toleration, once won, was evidently possible again, and its final achievement came seventeen years later. Uniformity was thus a fading hope and tolerance a rising ideal, which suited well with the new interests of the age. For the world had grown weary of dogmatists, and the great religious struggle was now a drawn game. The last and greatest of the wars of religion, that of the Thirty Years in and round Germany, had ended, in 1648, in a compromise whereby each side abandoned the prospect of crushing the other's creed or lessening its territories. Henceforth for a while the intelligence that for a century and a half had been devoted to controversy turned to natural science, which ignored the limitations of Churches, or to a neutral philosophy of mind. John Locke in England had rivals of like spirit to his own in France and Germany, and Sir Isaac Newton represented among us a movement that was general in civilized Europe. Neither of them sympathized with the dogmatic spirit of the generation before him. Comprehension was the object that the rising school set before itself. For in defiance of the dominant Laudianism in the Church and of the rigid Calvinism among Dissenters, as they must now be called, the new spirit was now at work among religious thinkers. Differences were coming to seem less serious in the eyes of leading men, and the seed of this change, which ripened in the eighteenth century, were sown in the reign of Charles II. The desire for a compromise was naturally keenest among the Presbyterians, for whom a national Church was part of the Divine order. Such a national Church stood before their eyes, and they longed for a place in it. If it would meet them half-way, they would modify their conditions of adherence. They soon recognized that they had made a grotesque blunder in insisting at the Savoy Conference of 1661 on a complete surrender of the churchmen to their desires. They were now obviously the weaker party, and with pathetic earnestness,

Baxter, their leader, framed plans of conciliation by which his followers might return without loss of honour. We need not be sorry that the negotiations failed, though a very few grains of wisdom in his opponents would have won Baxter himself.

But the reign of the Stuarts was to end amid a sudden emergence of the older motives. King James II violated the law and strained to breaking-point a faith in Divine Right which the clergy had pressed to a Byzantine servility. He incurred the loss of his throne on behalf of a Church which welcomed his downfall. For Rome was again as political as in the days of the Renaissance, and regarded James less as a champion of the faith than as an ally of Louis XIV, whose dominance was resented by the Pope as that of Philip II had been resented in the days of Mary. James was ruined by the delusion that it was still possible to dictate its religion to a nation; the Laudian party was to be driven, in this collapse of the old ideas, into an impotent secession.

CHAPTER VII

THE EIGHTEENTH CENTURY

FOR the purposes of Church history the eighteenth century begins with the Revolution of 1689, from which time Laudianism steadily decays. No period has been so systematically misrepresented. It is commonly asserted and widely believed that degeneracy of the Church was the cause of a degradation of morals. Morals were no worse than they had been from Elizabeth to Charles II. It is said that the stage and literature were impure. They were exactly as they

had been under Charles I and Charles II. Abuses
of non-residence and plurality are regarded as characteristic of the century. They were just as prevalent
in the seventeenth, being part of the inheritance taken
over by Parker and his successors, archbishops of
Canterbury, from the Pope, and uniformly administered
throughout the whole period from the thirteenth to
the early nineteenth century, save that the archbishops
made no such pecuniary profit from licences as the
Popes had done. To take one more example, the
severity of the criminal law is often charged against
the eighteenth century, and by a confusion of thought
against the Church in that century, as though it were
peculiar to that time. The law and the spirit in which
it was carried out had been unchanged for centuries,
and were to be maintained till Lord Romilly's reforms,
a century ago. Regarding the Church of the period
in this spirit, its historians have sought out and
chronicled its defects, while those of its predecessor
have been ignored. Three generations have seen it
with the eyes of the men of the Oxford Movement,
which was itself a phase of the romantic movement
of the early nineteenth century, best exemplified for
Englishmen in Scott. Now the eighteenth century
was not romantic, and was just at the distance from the
Oxford divines at which men's forerunners show most
to disadvantage. And those divines, like each successive ecclesiastical school and too many individual
clergymen, satisfied their self-esteem and pushed their
cause by depreciating their predecessors. To-day
that century is gaining rapidly in the general admiration
and growing picturesque before our eyes. Soon its
Church will share in this advance, and perhaps its
defects will be unduly palliated.

The men who took the lead after the Revolution
shared the spirit of the new and tolerant age; in

practice they cared for comprehension, in principle for benevolence. The former was once more to be attempted in vain. Tillotson's scheme, which would have admitted the Presbyterians and such Independents (a dwindling number) as were not Separatists, met too powerful an opposition among the clergy. Yet for a time vague hopes remained. Stillingfleet, Bishop of Worcester, was so far from regarding the Presbyterians as aliens that he entered into their internal disputes and did his best as a peacemaker, while the sympathy of Burnet and others was unconcealed, as was their recognition of the validity of Presbyterian orders.

The other novelty, the stress laid upon the Divine benevolence, was more important than this unsuccessful effort. The age was tired of dogmatic quarrels and revolted by the stern side of the doctrine of predestination. It turned for relief to the thought of the Fatherhood of God, in comparison with which it cared little for the rest of the creed. The new interest in nature that came with the growth of scientific knowledge took the form of admiration and gratitude. God's work was obviously good; men were optimists, and they would imitate Him by being benevolent. The Roman Church, in fact, had anticipated in practice the rest of Western Christendom in this respect; already in the first half of the seventeenth century its memorable works of charity had been organized. But in England benevolence was tending actually to supersede doctrine. This was especially the case with the Presbyterians, in whose eyes the Fatherhood of God came to seem contradictory to Trinitarian doctrine. They turned by a slow process to dogmatic Unitarianism. There was the same trend within the national Church, some of whose leading thinkers, such as Whiston, the Cambridge Professor, and Clarke,

Rector of St. James's, Piccadilly, taught a practically Unitarian doctrine. But this line of thought was carried to an extremity by the Deists. Reason and conscience are Divine gifts; God is good, and therefore His gifts are adequate for all our needs. It is presumptuous to think that more evidences of His nature and goodness are needed. Christianity is as old as creation, and everything in it that is not primitive in that sense must be rejected. But the thought of benevolence as the highest quality in God and men, and of the comparative unimportance of revelation and of the evidence of history, was not confined to those who rebelled. Such considerations prevailed also among normal churchmen and were to prevail so long as optimism could be maintained.

The Caroline ideals, inspiring as they were to their holders, could not maintain themselves against this new wave of thought, and they soon lost many of their best advocates. When in 1691 Archbishop Sancroft, five bishops and some four hundred clergy suffered deprivation rather than take an oath of allegiance to the new monarchs, which they thought was inconsistent with their duty to James, they not only deprived of a powerful support their sympathizers who remained in office, but also reduced them to an ambiguous position. In their own eyes, and in those of the public, the Laudian conformists had taken a doubtful course, and men in that predicament cannot argue boldly. But they worked bravely. London parishes have never been better administered than under William III and Anne, while the voluntary lay work of 'Religious Societies' and 'Societies for the Reformation of Manners' was powerful for good. The majority of the working clergy were of this school, and it was not their fault that the laity and the younger members of their own order were drifting away from them. Even had Sancroft and his Non-jurors remained at their head, the result could not have been different. The spirit of the age was too strong to be resisted. They were in a backwater, and though they might have freshened its current, they would still have been outside the main stream of English life.

But if the High Church cause, as it had come to be called, was a declining one, it made a keen struggle, which was as much inspired by political as by religious motives, against its opponents. There was rivalry between Whig bishops and Tory clergy for the government of the Church. The former were at a disadvantage in learning, for they had no one save Stillingfleet as a counterpoise to the weight of knowledge inherited by their opponents from the generation of Charles II; while as champions of foreign monarchs, William III and George I, they were unpopular not only with Jacobites but with a multitude who would not, though discontented, run the risks of treason. They were also hampered by the hostility of the Lower House of the Canterbury Convocation, for that of York, as usual, had little influence. William, whether or not he were a Calvinist, was a member of the Calvinist Church of Holland, and entrusted a commission of his Whig bishops with the charge of exercising his patronage, and with the composition of the injunctions which he issued, in Elizabethan style, to the bishops for their instruction in the discharge of their duties. This royal intrusion into the spiritual domain so irritated the Lower House of Convocation that the government deemed it politic to suspend the sittings. Under William, the Convocations rarely assembled.

Under Anne the Lower House was still turbulent, and caused grave trouble to her ministers. It had censured Burnet in William's day; under Anne, in pursuit of the same policy of attacking the 'Latitudinarians', as the Whig leaders of the Church were called, it made an attack on 'Occasional Conformity', which for a moment, in her last year, was successful. The Test Act had made reception of the Holy Communion, as an evidence of church membership in candidates for office, a legal necessity. The Presbyterians, among whom were many of the principal merchants who were likely to be chosen to such offices as that of Lord Mayor or Alderman of London, had no objection to compliance. In fact, compliance was in strict accordance with their principles, for they held that England had, as it ought to have, a national Church; they regretted that certain of its peculiarities forbade them to adhere to it, but they were glad to recognize its character by partaking at intervals in its most sacred service. When the High Churchmen raised this difficulty for the Presbyterians they had the satisfaction of censuring the bishops, whose desire had been to bring about a comprehension whereby Anglicans and Presbyterians might have combined in one.

But the chief cause of friction was a constitutional question. Historically speaking, a Convocation is but one house, for the clergy, like Lords and Commons, are one estate. But from early times the bishops and the lower clergy have agreed to sit apart, and the latter have found it necessary for the conduct of business to elect a 'Prolocutor', or speaker. But they are still one house; they meet as such at the beginning of their session, and again at the end if any canons which have received royal assent are to be promulgated. And being one house they have one president, the Archbishop; the Prolocutor, who is chosen by the clergy, cannot act till the Archbishop has approved his appointment. In fact, the Archbishop has an authority in the whole business that would certainly

have been attacked, and probably reduced, had
Convocation been actively and continuously engaged
on practical affairs.   This unity of Convocation was a
sad clog upon the ambitions of the High Church
majority, who did their best to raise themselves into a
distinct and co-ordinate body, with rights independent
of those of the bishops.   The Lower House would
then have stood to the Upper as the Commons to the
Lords.   There would have been two estates of the
clergy, and the lower would have neutralized the higher.
This case was urged with ability and passion by
Atterbury and others, and was conclusively refuted by
Wake, yet the Tory majority in Parliament voted that
the false history of the matter was the true one.   In
fact, Tory policy, with the Pretender in the background, was so intimately entwined with High Church
aims that when the brief dream of Tory domination
ended with the death of Anne, it was almost inevitable
that Convocation, whose Lower House had become
the mouthpiece, if not the tool, of a political party,
should suffer at the hands of the victors.   There was
abundant excuse in the acrimony of debate for the
prorogation of 1717, after which Convocation, though
members of the Lower Houses were formally elected
with each new Parliament, never met again, till 1855
in the case of Canterbury, and 1863 of York.   There
was no practical inconvenience to the government
in this suppression, for the Convocations, as we have
seen, had ceased to vote the taxes of the clergy.   And
we may doubt whether, in their exasperation, the High
Church majority might not have used freedom of
debate to implicate themselves more deeply in Jacobite
intrigue and so to alienate the nation.   This would
have been even more disastrous than the lethargy
which undoubtedly came to pervade the Church.
But since this was equally prevalent through Europe,

both reformed and unreformed, we need not think that a local circumstance, such as the silencing of Convocation, was mainly operative.

While the High Church impulse was growing weak, the preachers of benevolence and optimism were soon also a decaying force. One of the most overwhelming of controversial victories was that won by the Christians over the Deists in an argument which was worked out by 1740, the most effective champion on the side of revelation being Bishop Butler with his immortal *Analogy*. Now Deism was a form of the prevailing optimism; it preached the benevolence of an impersonal God. In opposing it the orthodox reasoners, perhaps inevitably, shook the current optimism. Butler himself was prone to despondency, as when he uttered his famous lament over 'the general decay of religion in this nation'. But it was not only the thinkers who were losing their buoyancy. Throughout Europe the same sense of sadness was experienced. The thought that all is for the best in the world, which had been current both among the religious and the non-religious, was ceasing to seem plausible, just as the optimism of Browning sounds hollow to our generation. Voltaire made it the butt of his satire in *Candide*, and so gave voice to the common feeling of disappointment with life. But there was a darker side to this reaction in thought. Men came to live under the fear of death. It was a topic which had an extraordinary vogue in the literature of the middle of the eighteenth century. Blair's *The Grave*, Harvey's *Meditations among the Tombs*, Gesner's *Death of Abel*, were among the most popular books of their day, and they are but samples of a whole library of the charnel-house. The earthquake of Lisbon in 1755 was much less terrible than that of Messina in 1908, yet while the latter merely excited a thrill of natural sympathy, the former stirred a deep and universal dread.

An England where men had lost their former optimism and were living under a shadow of fear, was ripe for a revival of religion. That revival was to be affected by the characteristic churchmanship of the age. Benjamin Hoadly, ultimately Bishop of Winchester, stirred up a strife which was called the 'Bangorian Controversy', from the see he occupied in 1716, when it broke out. No names have been too hard for him, but what embittered Non-jurors in his own day and High Churchmen since, was his success. He taught with wide acceptance that religion is a purely personal matter, and that Churches are only the unessential requisites for its organization. Far as the Evangelicals were from sympathizing with his cold religion, this part of his teaching long survived among them. Till the middle of the nineteenth century it was no uncommon opinion among Calvinist churchmen that all Protestant Churches and ministries are equally valid, but that, having freedom of choice, a patriotic Christian will choose the Church of his King and country.

Thus, when the Evangelical movement began, it found a nation taught in high quarters, and well disposed to believe, that ecclesiastical order is not a matter of principle, and that the law, laid down in 1661, by which ministration in English churches and the holding of English benefices is limited to persons in episcopal orders, is only a disciplinary measure. Hence it was natural that projects for reunion should be framed and cherished. That which has attracted most attention in later times was Archbishop Wake's courteous approach to the French Church, creditable to both sides and necessarily futile. But Wake was equally eager to meet advances from the Protestant

I

Church of Prussia, and was more nearly successful. The point of contact was the common interest of Prussians and Englishmen in the little Moravian Church. Early in the eighteenth century these 'United Brethren', who have an episcopate of obscure origin, were entering on the career of beneficent activity that has made them deservedly famous. The fact that they had bishops attracted English churchmen. Successive archbishops of Canterbury were their friends, and finally, in 1749, an Act of Parliament proclaimed that they were a Protestant Episcopal Church, and relieved them from the disabilities under which Dissenters laboured by law, though not in practice. Their piety was, indeed, of a type more attractive to the English mind than to the German. Wake's hope was to draw closer the bonds between England, the head of the Protestant interest in Europe, and Prussia, whose king was the Protestant potentate second in importance, by bestowing an episcopate, as inconspicuous as that of the Moravians, on the Prussian Church. Nothing came of it, for the imaginative king of Prussia died in 1713, before the scheme was carried out, and his successor was indifferent. But the influence of the Moravians was increased in England, and when John Wesley in 1739 submitted to their guidance he was behaving in the spirit of the normal churchmanship of his day. For the two societies which represented the Caroline tradition, those for the Propagation of the Gospel in Foreign Parts and for the Promotion of Christian Knowledge, subsidized Lutheran missionaries to Southern India, for want of English, throughout the eighteenth century; and though Moravians had bishops and Lutherans had none, there was a close affinity between them. And the fact that Moravians were Arminian encouraged the same indifference to confessional barriers among

English churchmen of Arminian mind that was engendered among English Calvinists by the teaching of Hoadly. Thus, when we turn to the revival of religion in England, we find in it nothing novel. It was a quickening of existing modes of feeling. The lines on which it advanced were already laid in Laudianism and Calvinism. The opposition between the two, whether we regard it as stimulating both or as neutralizing their effectiveness, was after the ancient fashion, and was never more strenuous than when the followers of Wesley and of Whitefield engaged in the strife. For the principles of Arminius and those of St. Augustine, as developed by the Calvinists, were incompatible. The history, as it regards the Church of England, is that of the victory of Whitefield's Calvinism and the elimination of Wesley's Arminianism.

John Wesley was brought up in a Laudian home. His father and his mother were of Calvinist parentage, children of sufferers by the exclusion of 1662. Both had rebelled against the grim predestination doctrine in which they had been reared, and the mother had even passed through that Socinian stage of devotion to the thought of Divine benevolence which was the frequent result of reaction from Calvinism. The son throughout his career, in which he passed through several stages of religious conviction, never hesitated in his belief in free grace for all. He was consistently Laudian in this. But he abandoned the rest of the Laudian heritage. He adopted, consciously or unconsciously, Hoadly's doctrine of the unimportance of organization. So far as it served his turn, he was loyal to his Church; when it seemed that an independent system would better hold his converts together he developed his own society to a point where separation was inevitable. And in reasoning out his scheme he came to the very conclusion by which the

Presbyterians had justified their nonconformity. He convinced himself of the truth of the Calvinist doctrine of the parity of ministers, and asserted that he had as good a right to ordain as to celebrate the Holy Communion. It is true that he exercised it to a very small extent, ordaining, in his old age, a few of his followers for the ministry of his society, and that he sincerely believed himself to be a loyal member of the English Church. But the whole tendency of his work had been towards separation, and his teaching on the nature of the Church, combining as it did the doctrines of Hoadly and of Calvin, would furnish reasons to justify the measure which his followers were eager to take. For Wesley, churchman as he was, had been quite indifferent to churchmanship in the preachers whom he chose. Few of them had been attached members of his Church before they joined him; many had been Dissenters, and he had excited hostility among the dissenting bodies by enticing from them, as they regarded it, their hopeful recruits. But most of the preachers had been rescued from a careless life, and their first and only religious interest was in the Methodist Society. Whether they had been indifferent or Dissenters, they had no bond of affection to attach them to the Church of England, and it was inevitable that they should desire to make their Society complete in itself, administering its own sacraments as well as maintaining its own discipline.

The schism was the more certain to come because no strong party in the Church held out its hand to Wesley and his followers. The Laudians, diminishing in number and weight, had no enthusiasm of their own that could inspire them to welcome the enthusiasm of Wesley, and his Laudianism on the point of Arminian doctrine could not blind them to his grave divergence from their general position. And outside the Laudian

circle Arminianism was regarded as error. Augustinian-
ism had the weight of tradition behind it. It had been
defended and expounded in massive volumes, and had,
it may almost be said, an œcumenical acceptance in
the reformed world. In the English Church there was,
before the Methodist movement began, an Augustinian
party, weaker than the dominant Latitudinarians and
probably weaker than the Laudians, but a party that
had a future before it because it threw itself heartily
into the revival of religion.

While the Laudian school needed to be resuscitated,
almost from extinction, by the Oxford Movement, its
rival, the Evangelical school, has had a continuity of
vigorous existence from the days when it recognized
and welcomed a kindred spirit in Whitefield. For
Evangelicalism means that side of the revival which
was hostile to Wesley and his teaching of free grace.
George Whitefield, unlike Wesley, started without any
keen appreciation of the Church to which he happened
to belong. He never had any scruples about Church
discipline, and was quite as much at home among
Presbyterians in Scotland or America as in his own
communion. He never felt the need of working out
for himself an ecclesiastical theory by which to justify
a change of attitude. From first to last the essential
thing in his eye was the system of doctrine that was the
common heritage of orthodox Protestants, and the
English Church for him was simply a member of this
federation of churches. Therefore it was a valid
communion, and therefore also it was Calvinist on the
point of predestination. When Whitefield first came
forward he found sympathizers among the clergy in
much greater numbers than Wesley, and there was a
steady increase of the school for a full century. In
1740 came his breach with Wesley, due to nothing
else than incompatible doctrines, for the two men

recognized each other's devotion; in 1840 the Evangelicals were dominant in the Church in England. Whitefield was at his weakest in organization, where Wesley excelled. The only lasting society formed by him was that of the Welsh Calvinistic Methodists, whose corporate strength may be attributed to Whitefield's abandonment of control over his creation. The Countess of Huntingdon's Connexion, the corresponding body for England, is a mere subsection of the Independents.

The Independents were to play a considerable part in the Evangelical revival. Their course had been straightforward; while the Presbyterians had diverged into the thought of benevolence and ultimately into Unitarianism, they had held fast to the Westminster Confession and the Calvinist doctrine. They were humbler people, less influenced by education and social position, and so immune from the influences of the eighteenth century. As an undoubtedly orthodox body, they seemed to churchmen who attached little importance to principles of association a suitable instrument. Hence, when Evangelical clergy, such as Henry Venn, Berridge and Grimshaw, found that many of their converts lived at too great a distance to attend their churches they encouraged the foundation of Independent chapels, not because they were Independent, but as a substitute for what could not otherwise be supplied. For the establishment of a new parish was practically impossible. It needed nothing less than an Act of Parliament. A parish was a civil as well as an ecclesiastical division, and the incumbent officially presided over a body which, since Tudor times and especially since Elizabeth, maintained the poor, repaired the roads, and levied rates which till 1813 were enforced in ecclesiastical courts by the penalty of excommunication; a serious punishment, for the culprit could not compel the payment of debts due to him till he had redeemed his fault. Independent ministers, then, served as what we call lay readers, and churchmen supported an Independent college for training such men; on neither side was there any thought of incongruity. It seemed right and natural that the clergy should so supplement their services. This feeling was equally strong among those who were content within the Church and those who were on, or over, the edge of separation. The Countess of Huntingdon, Whitefield's chief supporter, founded her own college at Trevecca for the cheap education of ministers either for church or chapel. So long as they were in earnest and soundly Calvinistic her purpose was fulfilled. Whitefield himself and still more his most vigorous successor, Rowland Hill, were on the border-line; Hill's 'Surrey Chapel' became a stronghold of Congregationalism. But whether they left the Church early or late, this contact with Independency led in the long run to a very large secession. The ministers came to attach importance to their own office, to feel that they would be more useful if they were their own masters, and to resent the barrier between themselves and their clerical patrons. Practical considerations, not theories as to the ministry, led to this loss.

But in spite of the secession to Independency of a great number of serious men, the Evangelical cause within the Church increased in strength. From the first it had been strong, where Arminian Methodism was weak, in clerical adherents. These steadily increased in numbers and in weight during the later part of the century, and secured a succession by gaining a hold on Cambridge University. From 1770, at the latest, the future was theirs, and their influence grew for two generations and more. They had no serious

rivals within the Church. Intellectual opposition
took the form, predestined to failure, of a revival of
Unitarian thought. The old repugnance to Calvinism
gave fresh life to an unbalanced insistence on the
Fatherhood of God. There was an agitation for relief
from doctrinal subscription on the part of the clergy,
which was unsuccessful and was followed by a secession
of able men in 1773. But they did not all secede.
There were bishops both in England and in Ireland who
were almost Unitarian, and they had many followers.
Nor was the Arminian opposition within the Church
serious, for the Arminians were either silent people
or followers of Wesley and therefore seceders. The
strife had been, in fact, so violent that it was practically
impossible for the two parties, or at least the keener
partisans, to be at home in the same Church. The
Calvinists won and the others departed. Yet there
remained, almost unnoticed, a multitude of quiet and
sensible churchmen outside the clamour of party,
such as Dr. Johnson, and in due time they were to
make their voice heard, and be the forerunners of
nineteenth-century reforms.

But the Evangelicals themselves were to undergo an
important change. They won their position by their
preaching of one doctrine; they consolidated it while
holding another. When the missionary impulse grew
strong, Calvinism was doomed. Through most of
the century it slumbered; the old societies of the
Church quietly carried on an inconspicuous work,
most of which was for the benefit of English colonists
abroad. But toward the end of the century all the
Evangelical communions were touched by the new
enthusiasm, and in spite of the resistance of consistent Calvinists, who held that God would save
those who were to be saved, and that it was presumptuous in men to interfere, each in turn, led by

the Baptists in 1792, founded its missionary society. The Church Missionary Society was established in 1799. This more humane view of Christianity led those who welcomed it into the paths of philanthropy. The Evangelical party has no more honourable names than such as Hannah More, William Wilberforce, and the Clapham bankers, whose labours brightened and elevated the life of the English poor and released the slaves.

Though Calvinism, except in theory, disappeared from the Evangelical mind, the domination of the school was not altogether for good. They despised learning and their contributions to literature were not marked by good taste or serious thought. As a body they were intensely conservative; this was, indeed, the general mood of orthodox people, for Unitarianism and Whiggery were closely allied. They were no reformers of the abuses of the Church, and they did little to combat the great evil of the age, the failure of religion to cope with the rapid growth of industrial towns. Too much of the ability of the school was devoted to select congregations in proprietary chapels, and the study of 'unfulfilled prophecy' consumed time that might have been more profitably spent.

In the externals of religion the Evangelicals made no change. We are apt to judge the century too harshly for its demerits in such matters as architecture, but our country only exemplified in a more moderate degree than some others a phase through which all Europe was passing. Against ugliness in this respect we may set the development of church music, in which England fully shared, and also the interest in church bells. The eighteenth century was the great era of bell-founding, and in it the art of change-ringing was brought to perfection. A further evidence of care for the churches was the frequent gift of good copies of famous pictures, and of originals that were at least respectable, to adorn the altar; too many of these have been unworthily displaced in favour of clumsy imitations of mediaeval work in wood or stone.

The abuses of plurality and the like must also, in equity, be judged by comparison with endowed churches elsewhere. They were symptomatic of the age. England was respectable in comparison with France, and if a few county families were founded out of the economies of Canterbury and York, they are insignificant in comparison with the stately palace, with corresponding revenues, that each successive Pope of the seventeenth and eighteenth century bequeathed to his nephew out of the savings of a brief pontificate. The clergy, as in all former periods, were drawn from every social class. Satirists have been too easily believed when they drew pictures of their humiliating position. What was true of many was not true of the whole body. The better livings were held, as before, by sons of the county gentry, by fellows of colleges, or by hereditary clergy, for many advowsons had belonged to one clerical family almost from the Reformation. A frequent survival from the century is a stately rectory, often too large for its modern occupant. For a clergyman who had influence enough to get one living often got a second; the archbishops still exercised without discrimination their Papal power of granting licences in plurality. But in parishes adjacent to these prosperous incumbencies might be seen glebe houses that were mere cottages, yet well suited to the social and economic condition of their modest occupants; while in many parishes the house had disappeared and the duty was performed by a curate, who might be waiting for an assured living or vaguely hoping that some patron would notice him. There is no doubt that, in an age which offered few openings for ability without capital or influence, many men took orders in a speculative spirit. They did not always adorn their calling; but certainly a career was open to men of talent. Far more archbishops and bishops in the eighteenth century were of humble antecedents than in the nineteenth. An unemotional England was in the main well served by men who practised and taught a Christianity that appealed by its very limitations to the age. Their merit was not the less that among their contemporaries were others, themselves labouring under limitations equally grave, who satisfied that emotional need of which mankind was becoming increasingly conscious from the middle of the century. It was to be the task of later generations to reconcile, so far as might be possible, the two standards of Christian service and feeling.

CHAPTER VIII

THE NINETEENTH CENTURY

IN England, as elsewhere, the French Revolution of 1789 was a turning-point of thought. After some fluctuation of feeling, the nation turned with invincible repugnance from its principles as well as its horrors. There was for a generation a recoil from change. Legislative reform ceased; it seemed that if a breach were made in the walls of tradition the fabric of society might collapse. But at the same time there was an increasing seriousness of thought, and a heightened sense of religion in those who were inspired by the Christian faith, and of the preservative value of religion in those whose interests were secular. The religious bodies, in fact, were bulwarks of society. It is the frequent boast of the Methodists that it was their influence over the working classes that saved England from the apostasy of France; and if this be only a partial truth they certainly co-operated powerfully with the Church in maintaining English Christianity and the English constitution. For the Church has never been more influential than then. The sense of responsibility raised the standard of clerical work, and if many of the laity rallied round the Church from a mere conservative impulse, they often came to be attached by higher motives to its life. One effect of the Revolution was that the clergy were held in higher esteem as a body. They were regarded as commissioned officers in the army of resistance to atheism and anarchy, and the social status of the humbler among them rose accordingly. We have seen that a large proportion had always belonged to the higher ranks. It was now assumed that all, because they were clergy, were on the same level. A consequence of this was that the humbler clergy decreased in number through the increasing desire of members of the wealthier class to enter Holy Orders.

The dominant types of teaching were Evangelicalism of the Calvinist type, which was steadily gaining in popularity, and the old-fashioned churchmanship taught at the Universities, where Evangelicals were in a minority, though at Cambridge, unlike Oxford, they controlled certain colleges. This older churchmanship was itself of two marked varieties. That which was the heir of the eighteenth century was at first the more important. It had been vivified by the fresh stir of thought and by competition with Evangelical fervour, but it remained cool and critical and had little reverence for tradition. Of this spirit were H. H. Milman, ultimately Dean of St. Paul's, who shocked many of the devout by picturing the heroes of the Old Testament as real men, and not as vague and typical objects of reverence. Such also was Herbert Marsh, Cambridge Professor of Divinity and Bishop of Peterborough, who introduced German criticism of the New Testament to English readers. Such also were the Oxford 'Noetics', of Oriel, against whose mode of thought the Oxford Movement of 1833 was to be a reaction. Men of this type, priding themselves on looking facts in the face, were often practical reformers in the Church and sympathizers with reform in the State. None was more practical than Blomfield, who died as Bishop of London. By his own activity and by his influence on legislation he was to be powerful for good. Among the devices of such men as Marsh and Blomfield for increasing the efficiency of the clergy was the revival of the ancient and almost extinct office of Rural Dean. If it has been less effectual than was hoped, it is at any rate a memorial of the zeal of the generation which preceded the Oxford Movement.

While these men looked to the eighteenth, the other school which opposed the Evangelical predominance looked to the seventeenth century. They were the heirs of the Caroline tradition, High Churchmen whom the self-sufficiency of their successors branded as 'High and Dry'. They were grave and well-read men, with a power of attracting prosperous laymen to their cause; Norris and Churton, Doyly and Mant were names which carried weight, and the Wordsworths added dignity to the school. They had many of the thoughtful and efficient clergy on their side, and the benevolence they evoked rivalled that of the Evangelicals of Clapham. It may be said without exaggeration that these two schools, replying to the Evangelical challenge, made the Oxford Movement possible. Education, missions, church building were in full swing before 1833; the life was there, and at the critical moment the Oxford teachers supplied a theory which gave an explanation for it and added a further stimulus.

Suspicious of both these schools, confident in their own position, marked, says an opponent, by 'spiritual pride and exclusiveness and obscurantist proscription of scholarship', the Evangelicals stood apart. If they attracted, as their best men, such as Charles Simeon, deservedly did, they also repelled. This was especially the case at Cambridge, where the scholars, led by Herbert Marsh, made the British and Foreign Bible Society an occasion of conflict. That society, founded in 1804, was among the chief evidences of the power of Evangelicalism. It proclaimed their principle that not membership in a communion but unity in doctrine was the important matter. The symbol of this unity was the Bible. The reformers had taken over from the mediaeval Church without examination its beliefs concerning the volume and its methods of exegesis. The only change was that with them the Bible was the sole source of infallible truth. The consequences were not altogether good. Bibliolatry can be carried to excess, and Protestant use of allegorical interpretation was often grotesque. But faith in the efficacy of the Bible, without note or comment, was profound. Benevolent men were eager to supply funds for its circulation, convinced that it would do its work even when thrust into unwilling or ignorant hands. They were the more willing because co-operation in this cause was a means of knitting together the different communions in a unity which transcended their distinctions. The scholars, on the other hand, doubted the competence of the multitude to extract truth from the Bible without assistance, and as churchmen they deemed it disloyal to withhold the Church's guidance from inquirers. The Bible, they argued, ought not to be circulated by churchmen without the Prayer Book as its companion, and therefore churchmen ought to confine their support to the society (the S.P.C.K.) which spread both together. The conflict was fierce about 1812; it is needless to say that neither side confessed defeat.

Nine years later the strife of Marsh with Evangelicalism was renewed. He was now Bishop of Peterborough, and used his position to attempt a deadly blow. He tried to cut off the supply of Evangelical clergy at its source. The party had recognized the strength of the freehold position, and many of its members were safely ensconced in parishes, while Simeon was using his own wealth and that of his admirers in buying up advowsons that his followers might have free scope. They were invulnerable, but it occurred to Marsh that if he refused to ordain and license men of their views, they would have neither successors nor assistants. So he devised a series of questions, described as a 'trap to catch Calvinists', which the Evangelicals could not answer to his satisfaction without renouncing their principles; for they were still Calvinists by profession, though not at heart or in practice. The men failed to pass his scrutiny, and at once there was a storm of protest. The Bishop, in reply to a question in the House of Lords, asserted that their admission would have been 'a species of toleration which would shortly end in the destruction of the Church'. His act was a bold one, for he was not attacking a struggling cause, but a powerful body, yet it was not the less ill-advised and futile. For he was actually imposing a new and unlawful test, and his flank was at once turned. Other bishops gladly received the candidates he had rejected; he had merely caused a temporary inconvenience and did not venture to repeat the experiment. Its significance lies not in what happened, but in what would have happened, had not the beneficed clergy had a freehold position. Bishop Marsh cherished no prejudice against the unbeneficed; he assailed them because they seemed to be within his reach. The freehold had protected the Evangelicals till so strong an opinion, among bishops as well as others, had grown up in their favour that it was vain to attack them even in their weakest quarter.

While churchmen were thus at variance among themselves a storm was brewing against them from without. It arose from the unwise patronage of Lord Liverpool's cabinet, of whom several, such as Vansittart, the Chancellor of the Exchequer, were earnestly religious men. They retained all the prejudice against change, and against any forces that might be regarded as favourable to change, that had been excited by the horrors of the French Revolution, and had failed to realize that the nation's will was set upon reform. They regarded the Church as a bulwark of the constitution, and granted out of a heavily burdened revenue sums of £1,500,000 for church building. The need was great, and the public augmentation of this fund was liberal, and perhaps, had it stood alone, the favour might not have excited opposition. But it was reinforced by measures against Dissent. Restrictions were put upon the activity of preachers, especially in the open air, and they were made to understand that the advocacy of religion outside the national Church was regarded with suspicion. Even the Methodists, a conservative body and friendly to the Church, were thus insulted, and it was inevitable that their resentment should extend from a misguided political party to the Church on whose behalf these measures were taken; measures which, unhappily, were approved by many of the clergy.

The attack was formidable. It was led by the

Liberal politicians, with most of whom magnanimity took the place of a creed; their religious ideas were largely furnished them by Unitarians, who had an influence much greater than their numbers warranted. The self-confident and youthful party of the Utilitarians, with whom their doctrine was an actual substitute for religion, was on the same side. In opposition to the promotion of religious knowledge they pressed the diffusion of useful knowledge; they talked boldly about the march of intellect, and strove to advance it by such means as the foundation of mechanics' institutes. But while these were the leaders, the strength of the attack was in the Dissenters, scrupulously orthodox and evangelical, who were incongruously yoked with them in opposition to the Church. They joined in it because the Church seemed to be one of the allied interests which undoubtedly oppressed the nation, while those interests favoured the Church as an obstacle to innovation. We cannot regret now that the Test and Corporation Acts were abolished in 1828. They had been annually suspended for a century, though it was still common enough for Nonconformists to receive communion in their parish church in order to qualify for office. There was no need for them to do so; it was a mere act of traditional kindliness. But the repeal was meant to be a blow to the Church, and was taken by too many churchmen as such. The same was the case with the removal of the disqualification of Roman Catholics in 1829. The Tories, and most churchmen, were still inspired with an unreasoning dread of change, and for a whole generation the pulpit had been used to inculcate the badness of the Roman creed and the danger of granting political equality to its adherents. By a strange sequence of events the Oxford Movement was soon to present Roman Christianity in a

K

new light to a people inflamed with prejudice and primed with argument against that Church.

But in the sweeping movement of change when Parliament and municipal corporations were reformed, the Church itself was taken in hand. What was done was in the main beneficial; but it was regarded as a succession of outrages by the majority of the clergy, and those who carried out the changes were openly pleased that while they reformed abuses they wounded feelings. Between 1832 and 1840 what was practically a revolution was carried out. Supreme ecclesiastical jurisdiction has been vested since 1832 in the Privy Council (since 1833 in its Judicial Committee) instead of in a spiritual court; in 1833 a number of superfluous Irish sees were combined with others, and at this point Keble made the famous protest which started the Oxford Movement. In 1834 began the agitations against church rates and University tests, which were to be finally successful in 1868 and 1871 respectively. In 1835 a Commission on ecclesiastical revenues, appointed in 1832, issued its report. This was followed by the Act of 1836, which created a permanent Commission with power (subject to life interests) of reducing or raising bishops' incomes and of abolishing a multitude of prebends and other cathedral and collegiate offices. To most of these no duties were attached and the aggregate revenues were considerable. The chief sources of income put at the disposal of the Commission were the cathedrals of Durham and St. Paul's, where coal in the former and the spread of London in the latter case had made what had once been modest endowments extremely valuable. The revenues sequestrated were ordered to be employed in augmenting poor livings or founding new ones, and the extension of church work in the poor quarters of the towns has been made possible solely by this means.

At the same time the dioceses were made more equal in extent and population, and the first measures were taken towards increasing their number, while power was subsequently given to the Commission to create new parishes by the cheap and easy process of an Order in Council instead of the old cumbrous method. In 1836 also another benefit was conferred upon the clergy by the abolition of the awkward and irritating system of collecting tithe in kind, and the substitution for it of a rent charge payable in money and fluctuating with the price of corn. The redistribution of revenues and the relief in regard to tithe, though disliked at the time as an interference, have produced none but good results, as has also the suppression of the immemorial abuse in pluralities and the enforcement of residence upon the parish clergy. Even more resented was the establishment of civil marriage, as an alternative to marriage in church, in 1836, and the grant of a charter to London University in the same year, which provided the old Universities with a rival where tests were unknown.

These changes had not proceeded far when the wrath of churchmen found expression. The attack was from the Liberals; the defence was undertaken by the most conservative element in the Church. A moment had come when the High Churchmen, with their veneration for the past, were the natural spokesmen. Great addresses from the clergy and the laity were presented in 1834 to the Archbishop of Canterbury, protesting attachment to the Church and determination to maintain its right. The feeling of loyalty was awakened. But a definite direction was to be given to thought by the leaders of the Oxford Movement who were the better able to give it that, with the exception of Newman, the most illustrious, they had been trained in the old High Church school. Keble especially represented that tradition, and had in him a strain even of the Non-juror. He reverenced King Charles as a martyr, and accepted without reserve the Caroline ideals in doctrine and life. He brought to the movement principles long formed, already expounded with great effect in 1827 in his *Christian Year*, and never to be modified during his life. But his opportunity came in 1833, when he raised his voice against the inroads of Liberalism in his famous sermon on 'National Apostasy'. Since 1832 Members of Parliament need not be churchmen, yet Parliament was laying hands on the Church, and in particular was interfering with the Irish bishoprics. This, to his mind, was typical of the spirit of the age, and his protest, according to Newman, was the beginning of the movement. The training and thought of Dr. Pusey were similar to those of Keble, and though he was more susceptible of alien influences, for him, too, departure from his Church was impossible. Newman's history was different. He had brought himself, by thought and study, to the point of view of his colleagues, but he had joined the cause, and on further consideration could forsake it. His affections were not rooted as were theirs.

Their attack was aimed not merely against measures but against a mode of thought which might be found within the Church as well as outside. The Liberalism of the day had its mild ecclesiastical counterpart. There were eminent men, especially at Oxford, who preferred reason to authority, held that many questions were open, and taught that we need only honour with a conditional acceptance views which in former generations had passed for absolute truth. Such was Dr. Hampden, the successive stages of whose career were occasions of strife. But the movement was positive also. It aimed at making religious life more real. Its authors were stern with themselves, strict in self-discipline, resolute to form themselves into the mould of the most perfect past that they could conceive. Thus they came into conflict with the Evangelicalism of the day, whose first enthusiasm had cooled and which had come to be, as Dean Church says, on very easy terms with the world. The new ideal of precise belief and scrupulous obedience conflicted with the earlier ideal of awakened feeling.

In spite of this sharp divergence there were common principles; each appealed to the Bible and to its own tradition. For both schools the Bible was infallible, though for the newer it had to be interpreted by antiquity. Among Evangelicals there was a wonderful knowledge of the letter of Scripture, which they studied as the sole and sufficient authority. But their reverence could not exceed that of such a man as Pusey, whose commentary on Daniel accepted without demur the traditional estimate of the book, and might have been written (apart from advance in knowledge) in any generation since Scripture began to be annotated. Neither side dreamed that within a few years the Bible would be seen in a new and different light. But each party appealed also to a tradition of its own. Whole libraries were hurried through the press to prove that the school which produced them was true to the past, and that its opponents were defying the best teaching of the Church. On the one side the patristic literature was laboriously translated; on the other the writings of the English reformers were collected. The men of the movement reprinted many of the Caroline divines to show what was the genuine Anglican doctrine, and when they diverged towards Rome the series was completed by the 'High and Dry', to show the obliquity of the very men who had revived the study of standard English theology. Every one took for granted that there was an authority in the past that must be followed, and was willing to be judged by his conformity to the pattern of his choice.

But it was the party of the movement that needed to justify itself, for it was advocating what seemed a new departure. In the series of *Tracts for the Times*, which ran from 1833 to 1841, and were Newman's own plan for the restoration of the Church, the appeal to the clergy was that they should rest their claim upon their commission derived through the bishops from the Apostles, and that they should take seriously the authority of the bishops over them. There was, indeed, great need for a recognized principle of association. Not only was there the combined attack of the Liberal forces from without; there was much unsettlement within. It was a frequent thing for earnest Evangelical clergymen to secede to one or other form of Dissent, and at the very time when the *Tracts* were being published the Plymouth Brethren and the Irvingites were drawing many recruits from the English Church. The principle of the *Tracts* was an effective barrier against such movements. But this stress on the historical ministry necessarily led to a respectful attitude towards Rome, through which that ministry had reached England. As we have seen, controversy against Rome, waged in a political interest, had been one of the chief topics of the pulpit for the last generation. The passion thus engendered, and with it the belief (by no means confined to Evangelicals) that the Pope is the Antichrist of the Apocalypse, were to create much prejudice against the Oxford Movement. On the other hand, Evangelical Dissent was now enlisted in the motley host which opposed the Church, and so the tract-writers might hope for acquiescence in a teaching which emphasized the difference between Dissent and Church.

The *Tracts* were vigorously written and buttressed with ample learning; it was impossible to ignore them. Consciences were awakened, and men looked to the past for patterns to copy. Some stopped short at the Caroline divines, and earnest clergy were to be seen walking abroad, as though they lived under Anne, in the canonical attire of cassock and shovel hat. Others made the Greek Fathers their model in thought, and trained themselves and their congregations in a rigorous and logical orthodoxy. Others, like Hurrell Froude, followed the very path of the Romantic movement as eclectic imitators of the more attractive features in the life of the mediaeval Church. They practised its austerities, believed its miracles—in the first stage of the Oxford Movement an Anglo-Catholic was apt to be more credulous than a Roman Catholic of equal education—strove to revive its observances and its architecture. They have a sad memorial in recklessly restored churches and grotesque stained-glass windows. But Rome was still in many ways mediaeval, and the old system might there be watched at work. It was inevitable that these zealous students of the past, animated with the practical wish of perfecting their religious life and work, should turn thither for examples. It was inevitable also that this should awaken resentment and suspicion.

But for a while the swing of the movement carried all before it. What seemed eccentricities were pardoned in men who were evidently breathing new life and strength into the Church. Yet by 1838 there was a deep cleavage, and the Evangelicals characteristically devised a subscription for a Martyrs' Memorial at Oxford as a test. The men of the movement refused to subscribe; and from that time we find an alliance between the Evangelicals, the conservatives, or 'High and Dry' school, and what soon came to be known as the Broad Church Party against the common enemy. Unfortunately for itself, the army against which they united was itself becoming divided. There was the majority, led by Pusey and Keble, who did not regard the Church as compromised by what they deemed the errors of its leaders. Yet these errors in its eyes were grave, and especially a plan, entered upon in 1841, for beginning an amalgamation between the English Church and the State Church of Prussia. The two were to have a common interest in an English bishop in Jerusalem, who was to ordain and rule the clergy of both who were working in Palestine, and was to extend his sympathy to various small and ancient Churches of Syria, which represented teachings condemned by the great councils of the fifth century. To the men of the Oxford Movement all this was utterly repugnant. The validity of their position depended in their own eyes upon the orthodoxy of their Church, and many of them had carried their mediaeval enthusiasm so far as to feel a quite Roman dislike for the Reformation. But the Evangelical Church of Prussia was a combination in one body of the two Churches which had sprung from the Reformation. It represented the errors both of Luther and Calvin; and now, in union with it, the English Church was to compromise its principles by friendship with Nestorians and Monophysites. In Newman's eyes this meant that the Church could not be trusted; Pusey was content to think that though its chiefs were taking a wrong course, the Church's character was unaffected by their policy.

While Newman was thus being shaken in his confidence, he was being led (in great measure by headstrong followers) towards Rome. The first step was that taken in the famous Tract Ninety. In it he argued that the Thirty-nine Articles, strictly construed, did not contradict the official teaching of the

Roman Church as formulated in the sixteenth century, and therefore were not a barrier against union, which he desired. His argument, as we now see, was valid. The Articles were carefully drawn so as not to exclude the moderate majority of their period; those whom they alienated were the zealots of the Roman and Puritan extremes. But they had come in popular esteem to be regarded as a proclamation of principles hostile to Rome. Men were prejudiced, and had not the knowledge of history needed to counteract the prejudice. After the publication of the Tract, early in 1841, there was an outburst of execration, led by most of the bishops, whose charges were, for once, important as guides to opinion. And incidentally the prominence of such a school as Newman's within the Church gave a fresh stimulus to Dissenting opposition. A definite doctrinal issue was raised, and it became clear that there could be no more such co-operation, and such indifference to questions of the Church's structure, as had prevailed on both sides in the later years of the eighteenth century. Enmity was excited by the emphasis laid upon bishops as necessary to the validity of a Church. But the bishops were as loud as the Dissenters in their reprobation, and in the bishops Newman had put his trust. His reasoning was made to seem absurd by their repudiation; and meanwhile he was coming to feel, no longer that the English and Roman Churches, essentially one, should amalgamate as equals, but that the latter, being the truer to the past, was the better of the two. The English was loudly repudiating his interpretation of its position, and Newman had not the patience, nor the indifference to logic, which enabled Pusey and Keble to wait and in effect to win. He took his own Church at what seemed to be its word; and he was so impressed with the duty of belonging to a Church consistent and positive in the statement of its nature and claims that he took Rome at its own estimate. There must, he thought, be a Church such as he desired. Rome claimed to be that Church, and no other made the same exclusive claim. Therefore, to the loss of all old associations and friendships, he made his sacrifice and became a Roman Catholic in 1845. He had many followers.

But in working his way to his new position he had made a momentous discovery. He had started as a convinced conservative. Truth was to be tested by the past. The ancient Councils were no more to be criticized than the infallible Bible, and the Fathers were to be treated with profound respect. Yet obviously the modern Church of Rome had departed widely from that standard. It was a chief delight of Anglican controversialists to taunt Rome with these discrepancies, and Newman had been active in the task. He had now to find a reason to justify him for recanting, and he found it in development. Doctrinal truth, he now argued, is not unchangeable. New light is thrown upon it, and additions are made to it with the progress of time; the test of them is their consistency (not their identity) with a former revelation. Newman did not frame the theory as a dispassionate inquirer; his sympathies had outrun his logical position and forced him to shape this novel hypothesis. Nevertheless, he has his place among those who have introduced into modern thought its characteristic idea of evolution and its interest in tracing the path by which things have come to be as they are. If the dominant impulse of the eighteenth century was emotional, that of the nineteenth was scientific. Different though their thoughts were, as Rousseau and Wesley were typical of the one, so Darwin and Newman were of the other.

The general condemnation of Tract Ninety and the subsequent secessions made the Evangelicals dominant in the Church for a generation. But the Evangelicalism was often allied with and coloured by a broader mode of thought than the earlier Evangelicals would have approved. Dread of the 'sacerdotalism' of the Oxford school drew the party towards all who shared this repugnance. We may take as a symptom the case of Dr. Hampden. In 1847 the protest against his elevation to a bishopric was made only by the Oxford men and other High Churchmen. In 1836 the Evangelicals had been among the loudest in denouncing his appointment to an Oxford Professorship of Divinity. The change was due to no alteration in Hampden's teaching, which had always kept well within the lines of the Church: it was due to recognition of the fact that he was an opponent of the Oxford school. For the most part the Evangelical bishops were sensible as well as devout, and left agitation to the rank and file of their party. But there were exceptions, and sometimes even the wiser erred, as did Sumner of Winchester when he repeated the mistake of Marsh of Peterborough. Keble was beneficed at Hursley in the Winchester diocese, impregnable in his freehold. Bishop Sumner refused year after year to ordain his curate, an excellent man named Young, to the priesthood. This time the error alleged was not Calvinism, but a doctrine of the Eucharist which now (so rapidly do standards shift) is a commonplace of the theological colleges. Like other schools before it, that of Oxford was saved from suppression by the security of the benefice. Bishops, representing the best wisdom of the generation that was passing away, though hostile were harmless, and the advocates of the new idea, when they entered upon independent parish work, could persist in recommending it to their parishioners till it became first tolerable and finally welcome. We may be sure that whatever schools of thought may hereafter prevail in the English Church, they will need the same protection of an assured tenure against the same prejudice of older men in authority.

The less official members of the Evangelical party did little for the advancement of thought or knowledge. Little indeed could be expected from a body which was swept off its feet into frantic terror at Bishop Blomfield's attempt of 1842 to secure a minimum of uniformity by requiring the use of the surplice in the pulpit, and ordering some few other changes in the conduct of worship. It is probable that if regularity had been at that time attained on the Evangelical side the opposite party would have submitted in their turn to a fixed standard of observance. But in 1846 Blomfield was compelled by widespread and sometimes scandalous resistance to withdraw his directions, and an example of successful insubordination had been set upon which the 'Ritualists' were soon to improve. After this episode the Evangelicals, apart from their steady work which does not lend itself to narration, from their philanthropy, in which Lord Shaftesbury was conspicuous, and from their expanding missionary efforts, which lie beyond our sphere, found their chief scope in resisting what seemed to them a Romeward movement. From 1855 onwards great sums were wasted over many lawsuits, which culminated in an attack on Bishop King, of Lincoln. That case, concluded in 1892, was practically the end of a series in which the party gained many more verdicts than they lost, once succeeded in changing the law in their favour, and more than once in putting contumacious opponents into prison. But they utterly failed to fix a maximum of ritual. By steady persistence the other side have now so acclimatized a multitude of observances against which the courts declared, that they have lost all doctrinal significance and are tolerated or even practised by good Evangelicals. And as to the points which still mark divergence, all serious men recognize the folly of penal measures, except in rare cases of petulant disloyalty. If the policy of litigation has been a failure in this respect, it was equally futile in the few cases where doctrinal issues were raised. Happily, neither side has been able to narrow the breadth of doctrine which since the Reformation has been the glory of the English Church.

On the Oxford Movement the effect of the secessions of 1845 was to distribute its activity over England at large. In Oxford its opponents were triumphant; in the parishes which its supporters held they could show in practice the strength of their system. Pusey remained in Oxford, the counsellor of the party, and was unwearied in argument and device. His chief strength must have been in the impressiveness of his character. Though he cared little for his own sake about externals and did his best, with small success, to restrain his followers from alienating congregations by novelties in worship, he was convinced that the mediaeval system of religious observance was the machinery requisite to maintain the temper into which he desired to train his disciples. He was strict to austerity, he inculcated habitual confession and exercised spiritual direction, he encouraged vows and was the first promoter of sisterhoods in the English Church. He was treading on new ground, and in his desire for the benefit of experience he made eager inquiries in Roman quarters, which were not always dignified and which naturally awakened unfounded hopes. Still less wise was the adaptation, in which he persisted in spite of warning and protest, of French books of devotion for English use. Those books certainly promoted the very result against which they were a precaution. Yet essentially he based himself on the orthodoxy of St. Cyril and the traditional estimate of the Bible. He had no views about development, and was ever vigilant in protest against successive inroads upon the immemorial theology which he and his friends combined with so many innovations, or revivals, in religious practice.

Widely though Pusey's influence was felt through recourse to him at Oxford, through his laborious correspondence and unflagging industry in ponderous authorship, it was through the interpretation of his followers that he was best known to the world. Wisely or unwisely, they advertised their departure from the common teaching by changes in the conduct of Divine worship. Ignoring their ancestry of ten generations, save for some recognition of the service rendered by those who broke from Rome, they put themselves back into the 'Catholic' position of the Middle Ages. Antiquarian discussions as to the relative merit of 'Roman use' or 'Sarum use', were among their most congenial employments, and their views were variously exemplified in the ornaments of churches and ministers. It was natural that this side of their interests should attract attention, and that it should be seized upon by opponents for attack, though every one recognized that the real cause of dispute lay in the ideal of Christian life that was finding its expression in novel ritual. But this emphasis on externals gave to the second phase of the Oxford Movement the unfortunate peculiarity that, of all religious efforts, it made the smallest intellectual demand upon its promoters. Experiments in ritual were easily made, and the attention they arrested was gratifying. Sometimes, as was inevitable when so many were attempted, they were absurd, and even though they were quickly abandoned increased the public irritation. But this general feeling only stimulated the innovators. In spite of the grave reproofs of their leaders they preferred to empty their churches rather than deny themselves the symbolism that they loved; but they did not fail to fill them again with converts to their own methods. There is no reason to think that the aggregate number of serious worshippers has diminished through the changes; it has tended to increase, in spite of irreparable mischief in some places and many wounds wantonly inflicted on devout feelings. For a certain hardness of tone has been the character of the school. They were harshly treated, and they have retaliated. The worst customs of ecclesiastical journalism and pamphleteering have been continued by a party which started with the singular advantage of being free from an evil tradition in this respect. Not that they were worse than their rivals in this matter, but that those rivals had the excuse that with them scurrility was hereditary. The new party has also shown itself peculiarly gregarious. From 1848 onward its members have grouped themselves into combinations for mutual support, which has often turned out to be a mutual encouragement against the desires of authority. They would deny that they supported each other against the law; but they failed to discover that secular courts did not bind them until they had exhaustively proved that from those courts they could expect no countenance. On the side of doctrine they have consistently asserted, not that their teaching is one that may be lawfully held in the English Church, but that it has exclusive claims to acceptance, and therefore they have approved the attempts that have been made to narrow the terms of communion. They were not guilty of the effort to exclude Mr. Gorham from a benefice, to which he had been presented, for the

offence of holding a doctrine of Baptism that had been
current, and even prevalent, since the Reformation.
But when that weary case ended in 1850 in the
conclusion that the doctrine in debate was tenable,
the second great secession took place.   Archdeacon
Manning, the future Cardinal, and his friends, finding
that the Church was more comprehensive than they
had thought, became Roman Catholics. After this the
party, though there have been small departures at
frequent intervals, has dwelt with increasing comfort
in its native communion.   It has attained to an
increasing uniformity of practice and to a widespread
influence.   But during the height of the conflict,
which was popularly known as one between religion
and science, its leaders became strangely despondent.
Intellectually it was for them a sterile period.   Their
conservative position had been stated in every possible
way, and all the resources of erudition had been
exploited in its defence.   Their topics were exhausted
and the force of their appeal was becoming spent.
Then, especially through the teaching of T. H. Green
at Oxford, a new idealism gained vogue, and by 1880
the movement took on a new phase.   It became hopeful, open to new ideas, more broadly philanthropic,
sympathetic to Liberal policies, and mildly rationalistic,
at least in the eyes of Liddon and his friends.   For the
new light upon Scripture had begun to tinge its
thought, and criticism was beginning to touch the
immemorial assumption on which its exegesis was
based.

That new light came to be spread through the efforts
of the third school of thought, that which about 1850
received the name of the Broad Church party.   As the
affinities of the old 'High and Dry' school, and afterwards those of Pusey and Newman, were with the
opponents of reform in the State, so those of this party

were with the reformers, and in both cases religious and political predispositions coloured each other. Arnold of Rugby, for instance, had a passion for social improvement and a strong belief in a Divine purpose that the nation, as an engine for the elevation of its members, should consciously be one. But this unity was broken by religious divisions. The Oxford Movement devoted itself to emphasizing differences and deepening them, and therefore he detested it. For he wished to see a national Church, including all Christians save Romanists and Unitarians, whose scruples would be invincible, and therefore he made it his business to demolish those principles, claiming to be Catholic, by which his opponents justified their exclusiveness. His friends of the older Oriel or 'Noetic' school, cool and critical men for whom religion was above all things rational, resented a scheme of thought which rested on tradition and went on to commend its case by presenting it in picturesque and imaginative colours. Soon the Oxford Movement itself furnished recruits. Able men such as J. A. Froude, Francis Newman, the Cardinal's brother, and Mark Pattison, revolted with bitterness; and others who had been attracted though they had not become adherents, such as Stanley and Jowett, came to share the same feeling of repugnance against this dogmatic and authoritative presentation of the claims of the Church. The recoil was proportional to the original stress, and exaggeration was often met in the ensuing controversies by equal exaggeration.

But there was a real advance in knowledge. Jowett and Stanley, in 1855, published commentaries on the Pauline epistles, examined from what was, for England, a new point of view. The consequence at Oxford was an unworthy persecution of the former, with a denial of the income he deserved as Professor of Greek. This

L

was honourably ended, as Pusey would have ended it sooner had his followers allowed him, but not till 1865. In 1860 a storm was raised by the publication of *Essays and Reviews*, a volume of papers unequal in merit, but which was justly regarded as claiming a liberty at least as wide as had been enjoyed by the extremer Latitudinarians in the eighteenth century. But it claimed this liberty on a new ground, as justified by additions to knowledge and advances in thought which had antiquated many accepted definitions and shaken the authority of many more. The meaning of this manifesto was quickly exemplified. Bishop Colenso of Natal published in 1861 a commentary on St. Paul's Epistle to the Romans which rejected the current exposition of the doctrine of that epistle. It was not a serious contribution to knowledge, and has had no permanent influence. His other work, an elaborate examination of the Pentateuch, published in many parts from 1862 to 1879, was a landmark in English theology. In it he adopted, and developed with ability, though often recklessly and in an aggressive temper, that account of the Pentateuch which was already, in 1862, widely accepted in Germany and is now generally received. The Mosaic authorship and the historical character of even the earliest chapters of Genesis seemed then to all schools in England an essential part of revelation. If they were disproved, the structure would fall. There was a storm of protest; for a moment Pusey and Shaftesbury joined their forces, and Bishop Gray of Capetown, using the liberty of a voluntary Church, gave effect to the wishes of a majority of the bishops and clergy in England. He uttered an excommunication which did not affect Colenso's legal status, and which was ignored by his English friends. Stanley, for instance, subsequently invited him to preach in Westminster Abbey.

There was, in fact, a steady growth of feeling within the Church in favour of less dogmatism. It won a striking victory in 1865, when the rigid Elizabethan form of subscription for the clergy, which ran, 'I willingly and from my heart subscribe' to the Articles and Prayer Book 'and to all things therein contained', was modified into the vaguer profession of a belief that the doctrine of the Church, as therein set forth, is 'agreeable to the word of God'. It is evident to-day that the question relative to the Bible at the ordination of deacons will undergo a similar modification. This widening of thought, more prevalent among the devout laity than among the clergy, was in great measure the work of men who did not belong, in an accurate sense, to the Broad Church party. Frederick Denison Maurice was one of them. The men of the Oxford Movement had no words of scorn and suspicion too strong for what they deemed his vagueness and heterodoxy. No one has so deeply influenced their successors. Maurice had no sympathy with Colenso's views. He proposed to resign his benefice that his protest against them might be obviously disinterested. For there was danger lest, in the anger of the time, men should be terrorized into professing more confidence in the traditional view than they really felt, and Maurice encountered with a noble protest the veiled threat contained in Pusey's demand that the clergy should 'for the love of God' publish their adherence to the manifesto he issued. With Maurice may be classed the three Cambridge divines who gave a new depth and accuracy and a new direction to English biblical and patristic studies. They turned their attention to the earliest period of Christianity. No longer was the developed system of the age of Councils to be the chief topic of the scholar's interest, for it was ceasing to be regarded as an authority above criticism.

That period for English scholars fell into comparative neglect, and the earlier records were searched as containing the material for the history of the Church's development. Lightfoot, Westcott, and Hort, especially the last, were influenced by Maurice. To them must be added Edwin Hatch, of Oxford. He did not succeed in tracing out the growth of the Christian ministry, but he indicated the evidences that must be taken into account, and set in motion an inquiry which will, however it end, deeply influence traditional views. The work of these men, and of many others, promoted an open mind; if it narrowed the area of positive assertion it furnished new lines of thought and new grounds for conviction. This service has been the more thankworthy inasmuch as criticism such as has already worked a revolution in our conception of the Old Testament has spread irresistibly to the New, and also to the earlier history of the Church. Hence, to speak only of the effect of these views of Scripture upon doctrine, or rather upon the proofs for doctrine commonly advanced, whole libraries have been antiquated and rendered irrelevant. The assumption upon which the classical exegesis was based can no longer be accepted without demur. But it must be borne in mind that belief is not held on any single ground, and that, among the complex reasons which have convinced Christians, scriptural proof, in the old sense, may have been made needlessly conspicuous because it could be easily put in logical form. Hence the opponents of this critical school have had no need to think that everything was at stake, and no justification for extreme hostility. The school, rather than party, of which we are speaking, has had a share disproportionately small in view of the zeal and capacity of its members in the administrative work of the Church. It has been suspected by the Evangelicals and the upholders of tradition, and overshadowed by the activities of the busy 'Good Churchmen', the fourth and last group who must be mentioned.

Bishop Samuel Wilberforce is their pattern, and in great measure their founder. He was a man of genius, and the tide was in his favour. When he became Bishop of Oxford in 1845, the normal churchman was the Evangelical. At his death as Bishop of Winchester in 1873, his school was predominant as it has continued to be, and the Evangelicals, though still important, had become a sectional interest. At the same time the men who represented the Oxford Movement had been shouldered out from their position as the main army of an advancing cause, and reduced to be somewhat irregular skirmishers on its flank. With him must be associated many others, such as Dean Hook before him and Archbishop Benson in the generation after him. They shared his success; they shared also, in some measure, the resentment of the Evangelicals against Wilberforce and the suspicion of the Oxford school. Their work has been effectual in the levelling upwards of ecclesiastical thought and practice: but, in spite of many adaptations, inward as well as outward, to the Oxford mode, no concessions have been made on that side. There has been no levelling down. Thus the success has been seriously qualified, and a central or national standard of thought and practice has not been attained, in spite of a widespread uniformity in externals and in the use of words; perhaps it is not desirable that it should be attained. The merit of Wilberforce, who dictated the methods of the Church after his day, lay in his inculcation by practice as well as precept of the value of work, not only as an evidence but also as a source of spiritual life. He was indefatigable himself, and set a new standard for his own order of the ministry.

His example, as well as his gift for stimulating others, excited in the clergy a new zeal for parish work, for cottage visiting, for manifold organization, for mission preaching. These methods, having lost the attraction of novelty, seem to be less effective now than once they were. But the clergy have attained through this discipline to a high degree of professional efficiency: and also, largely through Wilberforce's influence, to a somewhat professional habit of thought and outlook. In this respect the theological colleges have been influential.

If Wilberforce, by setting the example of activity, diverted men from controversy to more fruitful employments, it was not because he was indifferent to dogma. He was, in fact, the convinced advocate of a central doctrine, which he believed to be demonstrably true, and which was in his eyes the peculiar possession of the English Church. Therefore he was equally opposed to teachers who minimized the characteristics of the Church as unimportant when compared with the common heritage of orthodox Protestantism, and to those who regarded Rome or the Middle Ages as a pattern which men should adopt as their guide. There might be a judicious imitation of some of their methods, but it must be in no spirit of self-depreciation. Rather must men be thankful and proud that they belonged to a Church that was pure and primitive and efficient. With the same confidence he confronted doubt and all that suggested it. His first campaign in this direction, against the appointment of Hampden to the see of Hereford, ended in ignominy; he was more successful, for the moment, against *Essays and Reviews* and Bishop Colenso. But his chief efforts were against such advances in natural science as seemed to cast doubt upon current theological views. He is largely responsible, in the so-called conflict between religion and science, for the methods of scorn and ridicule that were employed by the older school. Yet the mischief he did was far more than compensated by the spirit of energy that he diffused and by his own achievements. His gift for management, which made him the dictator of the episcopate in his day, found an opportunity in Convocation, the revival of which in 1855 was in great measure his work, and every organization of the Church was stimulated by him. Such a man naturally magnified his office, and gained for it an increase of respect from the public. That cult of bishops as such, apart from their personal qualities or the importance of their sees, which perhaps reached its climax at the Lambeth Conference of 1898, was a new phenomenon of the latter half of the nineteenth century.

But the successive conferences of bishops at Lambeth, though at first regarded with doubt, have been so wisely conducted that they have undoubtedly guided opinion at home and tended to the unity of the Church throughout the world. They have been held at intervals of ten years since 1867, and on each occasion the number of bishops present—none other are invited—has increased. This growth of the episcopate, though it has been more rapid in proportion than that of their flocks, has yet indicated a substantial growth of the communion. But only in Australia and New Zealand, among communities of English descent, are churchmen relatively as numerous as in England. In Canada they are fewer than the Methodists; in the United States they are somewhat insignificant in number, though considerable in influence. It is often said that this is the result of the denial of bishops to the colonies in the eighteenth century. But the Roman Catholics had none, even after bishops had been consecrated for our American communion in

1784 and 1787; and it is almost certain that the revolution which founded the United States would have broken out even earlier had English ministers consented to the establishment of episcopacy, which was associated in the mind of New England with persecutions of the seventeenth century. Missions among the heathen have shared in the remarkable success which has marked all such efforts for more than a century past.

The dominance of the 'Good Churchmen', commended by the great example of Wilberforce, still continues. But their teaching, like their practice, had been increasingly coloured by the influence of the Oxford school; so much so, that in many cases, if the antecedents were unknown, it would be impossible to determine whether the lineage were from Wilberforce or from Pusey. The pride in a central position, as clearly marked off from Rome as from Geneva, has often disappeared. At the same time extremer men, sometimes claiming Roman examples as the sanction for their procedure and doctrine, are as conspicuous as ever, while on the other wing Evangelicalism is earnest and influential, if not so dogmatic as once it was. With general approval many practical reforms have been achieved; abuses in regard to the patronage of churches have been remedied, and inefficient clergy are more easily displaced. The clergy have never been more active or better supported by the work and the wealth of the laity. An increasing amount of this support is being devoted to the education of recruits for the clerical body; at present only half of the clergy have passed through the older Universities, and the problem of training a multitude of candidates, part of whose maintenance, if not the whole, must be provided for them, is being so seriously considered that we may soon hope for a happy solution. Convocations, Houses of Laymen, Church Congresses and other assemblages, not to speak of a copious literature, testify to a vivid interest in the welfare of the Church. On the other hand, a great change in English society has released the indifferent from the duty, which respectability laid upon them a generation ago, of attendance at church. At the same time the mass of working people who have never, since the industrial revolution of the eighteenth century crowded them into towns, formed the habit of Sunday worship, have not been moved by the efforts made on their behalf. The aggregate number of the devout among them is happily considerable, yet they are but units in the multitude. However, in spite of disappointments, good work has had good results, and the appeal of Christ has been heard. Never, indeed, has the interest in religion, though not always in organized religion, been keener than it is to-day. It shows itself in a philanthropy, directly inspired by religion, which is ceasing to patronize those whom it benefits. It shows itself also in the general recognition of the importance, as a necessary part of Christian life, of missions to the non-Christian world. It shows itself in a widespread interest in the psychology of religion, its bases and its phenomena. All these lines of thought have begun to draw Christians together, to make the differences seem smaller than the common heritage. They are also having a solvent effect upon the more rigid and traditional presentations of the faith: and, even where the old standards are most jealously maintained, we may often find the position being defended by arguments which savour, to use the diction of the day, of pragmatism or modernism. But the substance of the faith is securely held, and the interest in history engendered by our universal habit of explaining the present as a development out of the past is leading our generation to attach a new value to continuity. If the explanations and doctrines which have clustered round the historic ministry are an obstacle to union, the fact of the succession which links the English Church to the beginnings of Christianity is conspicuous, and is to-day a magnet of attraction to English-speaking Christians.

DR. WATSON finished his book a few months before the outbreak of the War of 1914–18. The succeeding years have seen great changes in Church, State and society; we have lived in a revolutionary age and its violent pace shows no sign of slackening. It is impossible, and if it were possible it would be uninteresting, to give in a few pages even a summary account of events in the Church history of these years. Moreover, to attempt this would be to desert the plan of the book. The author aimed at commentary rather than narrative, at distinguishing the temper and the movement of opinion and action rather than at outlining a story. This Epilogue too must select a few of the more significant changes in the generation with which it deals, must try to trace their effect on the Church's life, the Church's success or failure in dealing with them and with its own primary concerns.

It may well be that a future Church historian, seeing this time in true perspective, will judge its most significant fact to have been that the Church of England, in that gradual and undramatic yet decisive fashion characteristic of English history, came out of a comparative isolation from the rest of Christendom which had, on the whole, prevailed during the two preceding centuries. The causes of this movement were many. The War of 1914–18, the troubled peace, the renewal of war, the dawn of the atomic age, the deep cleavage between Communism and its adversaries, the surge of nationalism in Africa, Asia and elsewhere, altered the whole frame of the world's life. There were new and hitherto unimagined possibilities of progress, but there was also the continuing fear that the gifts of science might be used for the destroying of civilization. Fundamental questions about the bearing of Christian faith upon public and private life were reopened. All this combined to force upon the churches the need for common inquiry and for common action. But there were many other causes at work independent, or partly independent, of the wars and their consequences. The world had grown rapidly smaller; the fate and fortunes of its various peoples were seen to be inter-locked. The immense expansion of missionary work, which until 1939 continued despite all hindrances, revealed ever more clearly the need and the difficulty of united church action. Again, in a different field, English Churchmen were drawn to concern them-selves with new movements in Continental theology and worship, both Reformed and Roman. Karl Barth's work, though no doubt seldom understood and, if understood, generally critically received, has deeply influenced many who were, in any case, in-clined to react from the 'Liberal theology' characteristic of pre-war days and now for a time in the trough of the wave. If Barth and other Reformed theologians have stirred new appreciation of often neglected elements in the Christian heritage, it is no less certain that some movements within the Church of Rome directed towards fuller popular participation in worship and towards the remoulding of modern industrial life on the basis of Christian principle have aroused interest and sympathy in the minds of many English Church-men. Stronger still than the influence of these developments has been the attraction exercised by the revived interest in the Thomist theology. Nor was it surprising that, at a time when Anglican thought about the nature and functions of the Christian Church was stirred by the threatening aspect of the times at home and abroad, there should be a growing desire to understand the history and the present policy of the Roman Church, whose international position and wide connexions bring so unrivalled an experience.   There has, of course, been no reasonable expectation before or since the conversations at Malines (1921–26), when Anglican and Roman theologians met in conference under Cardinal Mercier's presidency, that any measure of reunion is within sight.   All that is noted here is a renewal of interest, and of better instructed sympathy with some aspects of Roman theology and Church life. And this was characteristic of these years of menace to Christendom.   Characteristic, too, was a revival of 'fundamentalism' in more forms than one.   In a world where so much that had seemed stable was shaken to the depths, it was not surprising that men should look for rigid certainties to which they could cling.   Biblical criticism has never been more active than in the last half-century, but its methods and principles still meet with vigorous resistance or at least with strong suspicion.

The need for reforms which might equip the Church of England to carry out its tasks more effectively was urgently pressed during the course of the War of 1914–18, and the active Churchmen who, with the steadying hand of Archbishop Davidson, brought the Church Assembly into being by the Enabling Act of 1919, and with it gave statutory powers to Diocesan Conferences and Parochial Church Councils, have without doubt given vigorous and continuing impetus to developments which are still very diversely judged. Under the old system legislation necessary to the welfare and efficiency of the Church was subject to intolerable delays, for Parliament grew ever busier, and many members knew little and thought little of ecclesiastical concerns.   There was little lay and not much clerical interest in the proceedings of Convocation, cumbered as they were and are by antiquated procedure and a too conservative constitution.   Church

Congresses aroused intermittent and sometimes useful debate, but they had no powers. And powers were needed, for in a hundred ways the Church's work was hampered by the slow inadequacy of its machinery. No criticism of the new system can rightly forget the positive necessities which stimulated its creation, nor the amount of useful detailed legislation which it has made possible. Some hundred and thirty measures have been passed. Dioceses have been divided and new sees created. Pensions have been provided for the clergy, at great cost: they are still inadequate, but a good foundation is laid. Cathedral authorities have been helped to frame new statutes and to equip themselves better to face the growing difficulties and opportunities of our times. Better provisions has been made for dealing with parsonage houses, their sale and repair, with the union of benefices, and the creation of new parishes. The Church of England now has a budget and an annual income of its own, supported by Diocesan quotas, and controlled by the Church Assembly through its financial executive, the Central Board of Finance. It would be easy to add to this list of reforms. Many of them have been generally welcomed. Yet the Assembly and the lesser bodies in Diocese and Parish have disappointed some perhaps exaggerated hopes. They have, indeed, brought the laity into closer touch with Church administration. This was a great need. But the lay members of the Assembly and of Diocesan Conferences alike are still commonly drawn fron too limited sections of the community: young men and women have seldom been among them: the electorate reveals the common tendency of Englishmen to cling to familiar and trusted representatives too long, and the absence, fortunate in itself, of vigorous party conflict in elections has the less fortunate result that many votes are not recorded.

Again, though a later generation will almost certainly conclude that the new constitution brought real benefit to the mass of the clergy and removed some patent weaknesses, this achievement has inevitably brought too an increase of centralized government. This is sometimes viewed with dislike. But without the help of the central bodies the work of the Church could not now be carried on effectively. Since 1948 the Church Commissioners have exercised all the functions which formerly belonged to the Ecclesiastical Commissioners and to Queen Anne's Bounty. Wise administration has led to a great increase of income and has enabled growing contribution to Diocesan Stipend Funds held for the benefit of those who have the cure of souls in the parishes. In many other ways the Commissioners have strengthened and stimulated financial advance during years when, owing to the rise of prices and the fall in the value of the pound, the need to increase stipends has been most pressing. And meanwhile the Central Board of Finance of the Church Assembly has deserved and won the growing confidence of the dioceses, who support it by an annual quota. The great need now is for far larger and more regular financial support from Churchmen generally, and vigorous efforts are being made, centrally and locally, to bring home the fact that the generous endowments of the past, however skilfully administered, cannot meet the demands of the present.

There is, however, despite growing co-operation and understanding between the 'centre' and the dioceses and parishes, lively criticism of any measure which seems to trench upon the parson's freehold. History has illustrated the importance and the value of this freehold. But it should not be impossible to preserve it in essence by adequate legal safeguards while at the same time recognizing the reasonable demands of efficiency. One of these is the need for greater mobility: this is hampered by anomalies, still considerable though diminishing, in the remuneration of the clergy, and by the continuing burden of too many over-large parsonage houses. Yet it may fairly be urged that these thorny problems, though still far from solution, are being actively considered, and that considering the distractions of recent years, the great expenditure of time and energy upon the abortive attempt at Prayer Book reform, the pressure of emergency legislation during the Second World War, and the long labours upon Canon Law revision, the record of solid achievement is creditable.

It should be remembered too that twice during our period the Church had to accept and face the consequences of the settlement by the State of two great controversial questions concerned, one with the Welsh Church, the other with tithe. On the whole they were wisely settled, but the material loss was heavy. The disestablishment and partial disendowment of the Church in Wales by an Act of 1914 which, owing to the war, did not take effect until 1920, has led Welsh Churchmen to turn their necessity to gain. Their new Constitution is steadily justifying the labour of its making: financial needs have been efficiently met: two new dioceses, Swansea and Brecon, and Monmouth, have been formed. The formularies and canon law of the Church of England as they were in 1920 are retained, and the Archbishops of Canterbury and York are members of the Supreme Court of Appeal for the Church in Wales. The once united Churches still work closely together. As for tithe, the abolition of the rent charge in 1936 has marked the end of an agitation which, however unreasonable, was harmful to the Church. The tithe owner will for sixty years from 1936 pay a redemption annuity to the State: the

Church receives redemption stock. Existing life interests of incumbents are respected, but the average decrease in the value of benefices hitherto dependent upon tithe may be reckoned at twenty per cent. This loss has caused and still causes serious anxieties: yet, on a long view, the Act was justified.

It is none the less true that many formidable and some pressing questions have not yet found an answer. The creation of the Church Assembly, together with the institution of an electoral roll for each parish based upon a baptismal franchise and a declaration of membership of the Church of England (and non-membership of any religious body not in communion with that Church), has undoubtedly given the Established Church a more denominational character. Hooker's ideal for the national Church is at last plainly disallowed. The Church has become more self-conscious. There have naturally been critical investigations of its proper relation to the State, many suggestions that the State appointment of bishops is dangerous if not indefensible, many endeavours to devise a more acceptable system of Church Courts. Valuable reports have been published, dealing with these subjects: facts and proposals have been clearly set out. The debates on Canon Law revision in Convocation have gradually revealed increasing unity in the Church on many matters: if this unity can be maintained and strengthened in dealing with the crucial question of 'Lawful authority', and if Convocation (with the support of the House of Laity of the Church Assembly) can thus present a solid front when its proposals are submitted to the Crown, there is hope that the Church may be given the larger liberty which it needs for the proper control of its affairs. But there are still lions in the path, and no one can guess with any certainty the future attitude of Parliament towards

M

matters upon which its decision is required. It is true that the vast majority of Church Assembly measures have been accepted by Parliament without any demur, after examination and report by the Ecclesiastical Committee (composed of thirty members drawn from both Houses). But Parliament retains the full right to debate and reject a measure, and no measure can receive the Royal Assent until Parliament has passed a resolution directing that it shall be presented to Her Majesty. The discussions on the Prayer Book plainly showed that Parliament will, if it thinks fit, exercise that right. It is likely that any measure dealing, for example, with important changes in the relation of Church and State (including the appointment of bishops), or any drastic disciplinary measure, or a measure directed against private patronage, would have to face heavy Parliamentary weather.

Even in this brief review the Prayer Book controversy and its consequences cannot be passed over with a mere reference or two. Its significance is relevant here, because better ordering of the public worship fo the Church, together with a satisfactory solution of questions of Establishment, patronage, and the like, still remain among the tasks of the future. Few informed people doubted, or doubt, the need for changes in the Book of Common Prayer, or at least for properly regulated alternatives to certain parts of it. About many of the changes finally proposed in 1928, after minute and lengthy discussion through many years, there was little dispute, and indeed, outside the circle of experts, little debate. The storm arose over the proposals for a new Order of Holy Communion (alternative to that of 1662) and in particular over provisions for the Reservation of the Sacrament. Anglo-Catholics were divided in their views: some welcomed alteration which, they believed, enriched the book and restored some of the losses suffered at the Reformation: others disliked them on liturgical grounds or, perhaps more often, because they feared that the bishops would be in a stronger position for enforcing discipline when, with the new book in their hands, they could better meet the argument that the legal order of public worship did not meet the needs of the time.   It has in fact been held with good reason that the effort for liturgical reform was compromised throughout by this connexion with the problem of discipline.   Evangelicals were in general opposed to the new book.   The general body of 'Central' Churchmen, the 'good' Churchmen of Dr. Watson's nomenclature, if we are to judge by the voting, were convinced supporters.   But despite the support of the Diocesan Conferences, and of all but a handful of the bishops, it cannot be said that there was real enthusiasm behind the new book in the Anglican body at large.   Therefore it is not surprising (though many at the time were surprised) that an alliance between the more extreme Anglo-Catholics and the main body of Evangelicals, backed by the old fear of Rome, led to the defeat of the measure in the Commons after it had passed the Lords. It was reintroduced, with some changes which alienated many Anglo-Catholic supporters without reconciling Evangelicals.   But it was again defeated in the Commons, before whom it was on this occasion laid first.   The debates had been vigorous, though it would be untrue to say that the debaters were in general well informed.   Public interest, in these last stages, was widely aroused.   The verdict of time will probably be that the Commons, if sometimes for odd reasons, gave a true interpretation of the nation's mind or prejudice.

The bishops made the best of a difficult and disappointing situation.   In general, they have regarded the 1928 book as marking boundaries within which variation from the book of 1662 is permissible though not legal. But liturgical chaos reigns. This does not mean that there is, or has very recently been, much active or bitter controversy in this field. The temper of controversy has indeed notably improved, partly because world events have compelled Christians to recognize a common danger outweighing differences. But the differences within the Church of England are nevertheless still deep. The great mass of the laity is indeed attached to no definite party, and though a considerable body of clergy, well organized and determined, appealing to a conveniently indefinable 'Catholic tradition' which is in fact largely post-Tridentine Roman tradition, pays little rsepect to Anglican formularies or episcopal rules, there has in the last decade or two been a notable increase of friendly understanding between men of widely separated ecclesiastical opinion. It may fairly be said that despite the liturgical chaos there is a growing desire for agreement, and a growing belief that ordered experiment along lines worked out by liturgical experts and tested by time and pastoral experience may achieve results far more effective and more satisfactory than seemed possible twenty years ago. Party feeling is certainly less strong and less bitterly expressed.

It is more important and more interesting to consider the tendencies of Anglican thought than the present position of the parties. These tendencies have changed markedly since Dr. Watson wrote. A keen and critical observer, with special opportunities for forming a judgement, has noted that in the dozen years before the War of 1914 interest was concentrated on the relations of religion and science, and on the historical foundations of Christianity; that the War gave a great impulse to consideration of the ethical, social, and political bearings of Christian faith; and that in the twenty years between the two wars there was a growing sense of moral catastrophe. This sense has grown still stronger since the Second World War. It is against some such background as this that movements of Anglican thought can best be observed. Historical criticism of the Bible, of the origins of the Church, of Christian doctrine, did invaluable work, and has much more to do, even if it creates as many problems as it solves. But it is no longer, as it was a generation ago, the dominant interest in the field of discussion. In Biblical studies it is being asked rather 'what is the significance of the Bible as a whole?' than 'how did the Bible come to be what it is?' Interpretation rather than dissection is felt to be the pressing need in view of the threat which comes from alien and hostile interpretations of life. There is therefore a demand for a dogmatic and integrated theology and an increasing attempt to meet it. Theologians are asked, too, to tell us what the Church is, not only or chiefly how it grew. An earlier generation was more content to study the manner in which Christian influences permeated society or were deflected by its many currents. This generation tends rather to stress the opposition of the Church to the world, to desire therefore to discover what is the Church's essential nature, what is its distinctive and characteristic purpose and teaching, what ought to be its relation to other societies and authorities. 'Humanism' and 'theological liberalism' have almost become terms of abuse among those who are profoundly impressed by the need for the assertion of doctrinal orthodoxy and for stricter principles of ecclesiastical action, and who believe that the last generation showed a too vague and concessive temper and that this temper is not yet extinct in the councils of the Church.

But there are already signs of a healthy reaction against extreme and sometimes fantastic attempts to assert the unity of 'Biblical theology' by methods of interpretation which disguise the varieties of outlook and approach so plainly visible in the pages of the Bible. Anglican scholarship still shows its characteristic unwillingness to allow theory to dominate or distort historical probability.

The vigorous movements of thought thus briefly indicated are apparent in many branches of English Christianity outside the Established Church. There as well as here the nature of 'Catholicity' is becoming a burning question, and many Protestants who abate nothing of their pride in their historic name are deeply concerned about the confusion both in belief and in Church order which weakens their cohesion and their evangelical power. This fact is important, both in itself and because of its bearing upon those discussions about reunion which have become so familiar. The relations between the Church of England and the Free Churches, during the period with which this chapter deals, have grown steadily more friendly and also more intelligent. If the Lambeth Conference of 1920 aroused hopes which are still far from fulfilment, it is none the less true that in forty years much has been learned, some obstacles removed, some set in clearer relief. Yet the present situation is not easily described. On the one hand there is much, though not enough, common action in social questions: there have been many joint declarations on a variety of subjects: 'agreed syllabuses' of religious instruction are in common use in provided schools: interchange of pulpits is more frequent than it was: the works of many Free Church scholars are widely read and highly valued by Anglicans. The Book of Common Prayer and the forms of Anglican worship have increasingly influenced the Free Churches: when Disestablishment is urged it is as often by Anglicans as by Free Churchmen. Both sides are alike affected by the contemporary 'climate of opinion' and by the struggle which is testing the Churches. Yet, for reasons that follow naturally enough from the change that has been described in a main current of Anglican thought, there has been a stiffening of mind and argument recently on such subjects as intercommunion and the doctrine of the ministry. Some of the declarations of the Lambeth Conference of 1920 and since have met with much criticism on the ground that they are held to express no clearly defined, or a definitely wrong, doctrine about the nature of the Church.

This criticism has had good results. Schemes of reunion now face a more instructed and realist examination than before. All parties are driven to discover and state their fundamental principles more clearly. They are increasingly unwilling to 'paper over the cracks'. At the same time there is ever-increasing desire for unity. The Church of South India is still variously viewed, but there is wide agreement about the value and distinction of much of its achievement and strong hope for its future. Other schemes, as in Ceylon and North India and Pakistan, have drawn both warning and stimulus from this first great union of episcopal and non-episcopal communions: meanwhile at home negotiations concerning reunion between the Church of England and the Free Churches and the Church of England and the Church of Scotland have been a constant concern. Lambeth Conferences have kept a watchful eye upon the whole field of 'Church Relations': successive Archbishops of Canterbury have each played an active part in promoting discussion, and Bishop Bell of Chichester made himself a master of the complicated questions involved: his volumes of

Documents on Christian Unity have become indispensable works of reference. The report on *Church Relations in England* published in 1950 has been followed by 'Conversations' with the Methodist Church which will be further pursued, and though the debate with the Church of Scotland has run through stormy weather there is no doubt that it will continue. No one can yet judge the probable issue of all these strenuous efforts. The Churches claim historical justification for their diverse views and principles, and in a book of history it must be said that historical inquiry has not found adequate grounds for disqualifying all views but one. It is safe to say that there will have to be wide agreement to differ on all except clear fundamentals, and after all the Church of England has much experience of this kind of agreement in its own history and contemporary life.

In these great matters the Church is slowly developing a more positive policy to meet circumstances which have changed profoundly since the time when the Church was the most important of educational agencies, and when, on the other hand, concern for economic and social conditions was based on a generally individualist theory, shown mainly by personal charity, and only rarely, in the mind of a few, developed into a thorough criticism of the prevailing state of things. Now the conscience of the Church has been more deeply stirred.

It would be difficult to exaggerate the influence in this and many other fields of the life and work of Archbishop William Temple, who himself owed a deep debt to Charles Gore. Both Temple and Archbishop Garbett of York, men of very different powers and character but both vigorously alive to contemporary tendencies in social and political affairs, presented the Christian interpretation of life with great force in books and by broadcasting. Archbishop Temple, a philosopher and a singularly clear exponent of considered Christian judgement on a wide range of affairs, was indeed one of the leading figures of his time: no English Churchman of modern times is more often quoted or more affectionately remembered. Since his death the Church has had to face an ever-rising flood of formidable questions. The coming of the 'welfare state', the shortage of clergy, new trends in education, the weakening of the influence of home life, the growth of divorce and delinquency, the need to use effectively new means of communication ('sound' and television) and to counter effectively their sometimes harmful influences, the vast growth of new housing estates with the consequent call for new churches and church-halls, the rapid changes in village life, the union of benefices and parishes in rural districts—this intentionally motley and miscellaneous list at least illustrates some of the prevailing anxieties and opportunities of the contemporary Church. Its active members, who are but a small minority of our whole population, are concerned to discover, in doctrine and practice, how the Church can best use and increase its spiritual and material resources to meet the deepest demands of a fast-changing England. This discovery must needs be a long and arduous task. The State has undertaken great new responsibilities: the Church has to learn how best to co-operate with all men of good will and at the same time to exercise a Christian and constructive judgement which must often, in the best sense, be critical. Both 'evangelism' and 'pastoral care' are still plain duties: the conditions under which they have to be performed have changed very materially since Dr. Watson wrote his concluding chapter.

This brief epilogue may well end with a reminder of what was written near its beginning. The Church of England, with all its domestic perplexities, is increasingly concerned with the work of the Christian Church 'dispersed throughout the whole world'. Its historic tradition, its 'Catholic' and 'Protestant' sympathies, give it a peculiar position, full alike of difficulty and opportunity. Its Archbishops, and such notable 'ecumenical' figures as George Bell of Chichester, have travelled widely and given Anglicanism many new windows upon the world. Our national Church has outgrown any narrow nationalism: it desires to proclaim the Christian faith wherever and whenever it may: it prays for the unity of the Spirit in the bond of peace.

BIBLIOGRAPHY

BOOKS originally listed by Dr. Watson, and others published since, include the following:

BEDE's *Ecclesiastical History* (several translations) and A. HAMILTON THOMPSON's study of *Bede*; MATTHEW PARIS's *Chronica Majora* (trans. Giles); DOM D. KNOWLES's *Monastic Order in England*, and *Religious Orders in England*; Z. N. BROOKE's *The English Church and the Papacy*; G. R. OWST's *Preaching in Medieval England*; studies of *Wyclif* by G. LECHLER (trans. Lorimer, rev. ed. 1884) and H. B. WORKMAN.

F. M. POWICKE, *The Reformation in England*, and G. CONSTANT, *The Reformation in England*; R. W. DIXON's *History of the Church of England . . .* 1529–1563; with FOXE's *Book of Martyrs* and HOOKER's *Ecclesiastical Polity*; R. G. USHER's *The Reconstruction of the English Church*, and *The High Commission*.

S. R. GARDINER's *History of England* (1603–56) and its continuation by C. H. FIRTH; CLARENDON, and BURNET, and numerous 17th-cent. biographies; C. J. ABBEY and J. H. OVERTON's *English Church in the Eighteenth Century*; N. SYKES's *Church and State in England in the Eighteenth Century*, and *William Wake*; JOHN WESLEY's *Diary*.

C. SMYTH's *Simeon and Church Order*; R. W. CHURCH's *The Oxford Movement*, Y. T. BRILIOTH's *The Anglican Revival*, and S. C. CARPENTER's *Church and People*, 1789–1889, with 19th-cent. biographies, especially those of Newman, Pusey, Wilberforce, Tait, Maurice, Benson, and Creighton.

G. K. A. BELL's *Randall Davidson*, G. L. PRESTIGE's *Charles Gore*, HENSLEY HENSON's *Retrospect*, J. G. LOCKHART's *Cosmo Gordon Lang*, F. A. IREMONGER's *William Temple*, S. C. CARPENTER's *Winnington Ingram* and C. SMYTH's *Cyril Forster Garbett*.

For reference, GEE and HARDY's *Documents Illustrative*

of English Church History, A. W. POLLARD's *Records of the English Bible*, F. E. BRIGHTMAN's *The English Rite*, OLLARD and CROSSE's *Dictionary of English Church History* and F. L. CROSS's *Oxford Dictionary of the Christian Church* (with numerous bibliographies).

INDEX

Abbot, George, Archbishop, 107

Aidan, St., 15

Alcuin, 20

Alien priories, 63

Alphage, St., 22

America, Church in, 167–8

Anabaptists, 86

Anglo-Catholics, 178, 179, 180

Anne, Queen, 125, 175

Anselm, St., 27, 55

Archdeacons, 52, 70

Arminianism, 111–12, 130–1

Arnold, Dr. Thomas, 161

Atterbury, Francis, Bishop, 127

Augustine, St., 8–9

Avignon, 62–3, 66

Bancroft, Richard, Archbishop, 99, 107

Barth, Karl, 172

Baxter, Richard, 121

Bede, the Venerable, 9–10, 40

Bell, G. K. A., Bishop, 183–4, 186

Benson, Edward White, Archbishop, 165

Bible, the English, 67

Biblical criticism, 173, 181; theology, 182

Bishops, 11, 13 ff., 22 ff., 29, 32, 34, 37, 69, 78, 83–4, 89–91, 139, 146, 167

Boniface, St., 20

Bonner, Edmund, Bishop, 83, 90

Broad Church Party, 152, 160

Bucer, Martin, 87

Bullinger, Heinrich, 85

Bunyan, John, 119

Burnet, Gilbert, Bishop, 125

Butler, Samuel, 128

Calvinists, 98, 100, 104, 111, 131

Canon Law, 50, 177

Canons of 1604, 105

Canons, 21, 34–5

Canterbury, 16, 17, 18, 23, 53, 55–6, 57, 59, 60, 62, 94, 176

Carthusians, 73

Casaubon, Isaac, 108

Cathedrals, 34 ff., 146, 174

Celtic Church, 12, 15–16

'Central' Churchmen, 179

Chad, St., 15

Charles I, 110, 119

Church Assembly, 173, 174, 175, 177

Church Commissioners, 175

Church Congress, 174

Churchwardens, 76

Cistercians, 42, 71

Clergy, taxation of, 31

Colenso, John William, Bishop, 162

Colleges, foundation of, 72–3

Comprehension, 120, 123

Convocation, 32–3, 42, 92, 105, 125, 167, 174, 177

Cranmer, Thomas, Archbishop, 53, 86, 87, 90

Crusades, 31–2

Davidson, Randall Thomas, Archbishop, 173

Deists, 128

Diocesan Conferences, 173, 174, 179

Disestablishment, 176, 183

Dissent, 119–20, 144–5, 150, 153.
Divine Right, 110, 121
Dominic, St., 45
Dunstan, St., 22

Ecclesiastical Commission, 146, 175
Edward I, 32, 33, 59, 60, 62
Edward VI, 84, 87, 89, 90
Elizabeth I, 91 ff.
Enabling Act, 173
England, Conversion of, 9, 15
Essays and Reviews, 162, 166
Evangelicalism, 129, 133 ff., 136–7, 140 ff., 149, 150, 151, 152, 155, 156–7, 179

Feudalism, 28 ff.
Forgeries, 52 ff.
Foxe, John, 94
Free Churches, 182, 183
French Revolution, 139 ff.
Friars, 43 ff., 73–4
Froude, Hurrell, 151

Garbett, Cyril, Archbishop, 184
Gardiner, Stephen, Bishop, 84, 90
Germany, Conversion of, 20
Germany, Reformation of, 80 ff., 85
Germany, Religion in, 64–5
Glebe, 10–11
'Good Churchmen', 165 ff., 179
Gore, Charles, Bishop, 184
Gorham case, the, 159–60
Greek Church, 109
Green, Thomas Hill, 160
Gregory the Great, 8, 15

Hadrian IV, 38, 59
Hampton Court Conference, 104
Hatch, Edwin, 164
Henry III, 59, 62
Henry VIII, 35, 43, 70, 72, 74, 81 ff., 101, 105
Herbert, George, 110
High Church Party, 108 ff., 112, 119, 124 ff., 127, 131, 141, 147–8, 149–50, 165
High Commission, 101, 106
Hook, Dean, 165
Hooker, Richard, 87, 99, 177
Hooper, John, Bishop, 88
Hort, Fenton John Anthony, 164

Independents, 96 ff., 113, 134
India, Church in, 183
Investiture, 55
Ireland, 59

James I, 103
James II, 121
Jowett, Benjamin, 161

Keble, John, 148
Knox, John, 88, 94

Lambeth Conferences, 167, 182, 183
Lanfranc, Archbishop, 27, 52, 54
Langton, Stephen, Archbishop, 55
Latimer, Hugh, Bishop, 70
Latitudinarians, 126, 129
Laud, William, Archbishop, 110 ff.
Leo X, 79
Liberal theology, 172
Lightfoot, Joseph Barber, Bishop, 164

Liverpool, Lord, 144
Locke, John, 120
Lollards, 68

Malines conversations, 173
Margaret, the Lady, 72
'Martin Marprelate', 100
Martyr, Peter, 87
Mary, Queen, 90–1
Maurice, Frederick Denison, 163
Mercier, Cardinal, 173
Methodism, 133 ff., 140, 144, 184
Milman, Henry, Dean, 140
Monasticism, 8, 9–10, 21 ff., 34, 37 ff., 71, 82
Moravians, 130
More, Hannah, 137

Newman, John Henry, Cardinal, 147, 150
Newton, Sir Isaac, 120
Nonjurors, 124–5
Nuns, 22, 40

Observant Franciscans, 74
Ockham, William of, 64
'Old Minsters', 10, 14, 25
Orders, 88, 94–5, 99, 107, 109, 116–7, 129 ff., 170
Oriel School, 141, 148
Osmund, St., 34
Oxford Movement, 141, 147 ff.

Paganism, English, 9, 10
Parish clergy, 11–12, 27, 29, 32–3, 38–9, 74–5, 101, 138 140, 166
Parker, Matthew, Archbishop, 94
Parochial Church Councils, 173, 174

'Parson's freehold', 13, 29, 106, 143, 155, 175
Partonage, 10–11, 12, 29–30, 76
Paul's, St., Cathedral, 11, 35, 146
Peter's Peace, 19
Philip of Spain, 91, 92
Pole, Reginald, Cardinal, 90, 91
Presbyterians, 96 ff., 113 ff., 120, 123, 126, 132
Prayer Book reform, 178 ff.
Provinces, ecclesiastical, 15, 31
Prussia, Church of, 130, 152
Puritans, 93, 96, 103 ff., 110 ff.
Pusey, Dr. Edward Bouverie, 148, 163

Queen Anne's Bounty, 175

Reformation, 77 ff., 152, 178
Reservation, 178
Restoration, the, 116
Ridley, Nicholas, Bishop, 89
Ritualism, 156 ff., 165
Rome, 15, 18, 20, 27 ff., 48 ff., 61 ff., 78 ff., 91 ff., 102, 108 ff., 138, 145, 149, ff. 157 ff., 168, 173, 179, 180
Rural deans, 52, 141

Salisbury, 35–6
Sancroft, William, Archbishop, 124
Savoy Conference, 120
Scotland, 59, 63, 96, 107–8, 183–4
Separatists, 97, 118
Sheldon, Gilbert, Archbishop, 33
South India, Church of, 183

Stanley, Arthur Penrhyn, Dean, 161
Supreme Governor, 96
Supreme Head, 82, 90, 96
Swiss Reformation, 85

Temple, William, Archbishop, 184–5
Theodore of Tarsus, Archbishop, 16, 19
Thomas, St., of Canterbury, 55
Thomist theology, 172
Tillotson, John, Archbishop, 123
Tithe, 23 ff., 36, 38, 147, 176–7
Tracts for the Times, 150 ff.

Unitarians, 86, 123, 136, 145
Unity, Christian, 183–4

Vicarages, 36, 38 ff., 76
Vikings, 21

Wake, William, Archbishop, 127, 129
Wales, 59–60, 176
Welfare State, the, 185
Wesley, John, 131 ff.
Westcott, Brooke Foss, Bishop, 164
Westminster Assembly, 112
Whitby, Council of, 16
Whitefield, George, 133–4
Whitgift, John, Archbishop, 73, 98, 104
Wilberforce, Samuel, Bishop, 165 ff.
Wilberforce, William, 137
Wilfrid of York, 17
William III, 124
Winchelsey, Archbishop, 33
Wolsey, Thomas, Cardinal, 72, 83
Worcester, 70
Wyclif, John, 65 ff.
Wykeham, William of, 64

York, 16–17, 23, 33, 53, 176

PRINTED IN GREAT BRITAIN BY THE RIVERSIDE PRESS, EDINBURGH
3½.61.